THE EASY
Puerto Rican
COOKBOOK

THE EASY

Puerto Rican

COOKBOOK

100 Classic Recipes Made Simple

TONY RICAN

Photography by Marija Vidal

ROCKRIDGE
PRESS

For general information on our other products and services or to obtain technical support, please contact our Customer Care Department within the United States at (866) 744-2665, or outside the United States at (510) 253-0500.

Rockridge Press publishes its books in a variety of electronic and print formats. Some content that appears in print may not be available in electronic books, and vice versa.

TRADEMARKS: Rockridge Press and the Rockridge Press logo are trademarks or registered trademarks of Callisto Media Inc. and/or its affiliates, in the United States and other countries, and may not be used without written permission. All other trademarks are the property of their respective owners. Rockridge Press is not associated with any product or vendor mentioned in this book.

Interior & Cover Designer: Lisa Forde
Art Producer: Sara Feinstein
Editor: Marjorie DeWitt
Production Editor: Matthew Burnett

Photography © Marija Vidal, 2020
Food styling by Victoria Woollard.
Author photo courtesy of © Ian Storck.

Cover: Picadillo de Carne, Page 123; Black Beans and White Rice, Page 105; and Guava Margarita, Page 21

ISBN: Print 978-1-64611-803-8
eBook 978-1-64611-804-5

R0

This one's for my dad, *Rafael*.
He may be gone but is in my heart every time
I cook for my family.

Contents

Introduction

It's all about making connections.

Like roughly 5 million people in the United States, my family comes from the island of Puerto Rico. I was the first generation not born on the island itself. My brother and I were raised very American; my family spoke English at home, and we ate a predominantly American diet. Still though, one of my strongest and earliest memories was my dad taking me to the Puerto Rican Parade and Festival in Chicago. I instantly fell in love with the music and the food—especially the food. It was later that summer that my tío Julio and Tía Juanita came to visit from Santurce, and my life changed forever. Juanita spoke no English but man, could she cook, and she was happy to show me how to make her favorite recipes. That summer I ate more Arroz con Gandules than I ever had, and it still wasn't enough. Once I got a little older, we started visiting family in Puerto Rico more often and those were some of the best memories of my life. Living on a beautiful tropical island for a summer, immersed in a different culture than I was used to in Chicago, my mind was blown. The best part was going out to eat with family where we enjoyed delicious meals inspired by the island. I remember going to a small restaurant where they had a pig roasting on a spit—that was the day I fell in love with pork.

Years later when I became a father myself, I realized I had lost touch with much of the culture I grew up with. My heritage was just something I remembered and not something that was a big part of my life, so I called my dad and asked him to teach me to cook Puerto Rican food. He happily obliged and began teaching me the dishes that his mom taught to him when he was a kid growing up in the 1940s. I was reconnecting with my past and heritage through my family's traditional recipes and in turn, I began teaching and connecting with my son through the same things. I began joining Puerto Rican food groups on social media where I learned that every family in every region has their own variation on how to make dishes, and not a single one of these is the right or wrong way to prepare the food. Families come together over these meals, and friends connect sharing recipes and cooking together.

After learning the traditions of Puerto Rican cuisine and cooking classic dishes, I started to add a modern twist to them, both in terms of the ingredients and the way they're prepared. In this book, I'll teach you how to make some of the most classic and flavorful dishes in Puerto Rican cuisine, with easy-to-follow recipes and simple ingredients you can find anywhere. While Puerto Rico's cuisine has so much to offer, the best part is connecting with your family and friends over an amazing meal.

1

Puerto Rican Food Made Simple

OTHER THAN A COUPLE OF CLASSIC DISHES, PUERTO RICAN food is largely unknown. Only a lucky few who happen to be good friends with a Puerto Rican family have tried a lot of the food we have to offer. So, before we jump into the recipes, first I want to bring you into my family and teach you a little about Puerto Rico so you can become familiar with our corner of the world. You'll see some similarities between what we do in a Puerto Rican kitchen and a typical American household. Some of the names of our ingredients may seem a little intimidating, or we may use a different word for a kitchen utensil, but I promise the cooking will come easy and naturally, and the rewards will be amazing. Puerto Rican food is packed with flavor and quickly wins the hearts of everyone who tries it.

A Rich Culinary History

Puerto Rican cuisine has just about as rich and diverse a history as any ethnic cuisine the world over. Originally taking cues from Spanish, West African, and Indigenous Taíno recipes, Puerto Rican cuisine also incorporates aspects from the vast diversity of other Caribbean countries as well as the United States.

In the Borinquen diaspora across the US, in cities throughout Puerto Rico, and often from home to home, Puerto Rican cuisine has been adapted and tailored to suit the tastes of each family and group of friends, customized to our palates using the *pilon* and *caldero*. The pilon is a wooden mortar and pestle mainly used to grind spices and mash plantains; the use of wood allows the food to develop its own flavor profile. The caldero is the traditional cast-iron Dutch oven–style pot that many Puerto Ricans consider sacred when it comes to cooking rice to perfection, while producing the gorgeous and flavorful *pegao* (the burnt rice that sticks to the bottom of the pan).

Puerto Rican food incorporates the vast array of local flora and fauna on *La Isla del Encanto* (the Island of Enchantment), from the national fruit, star fruit, to the staples of rice, beans, cassava/yuca, and *plátanos*, to the meat dishes where chicken and pork reign supreme. With its vast acreage of sugar plantations and tropical jungles where mango, pineapple, and guanabana are merely an arm's length away, Puerto Ricans are never far from delicious snacks. While the ingredients alone are enough to bring *la familia* running to the dining room, the gems of the Puerto Rican kitchen are sofrito, sazón, adobo, and the spice rack.

Much as Puerto Ricans are an adaptable people, so is our cuisine. Throughout this book you will see many recipes that seem similar to those you might find in an Italian, Irish, or Arab cookbook, except that these recipes have that Rican twist, swapping key ingredients from the original recipe for those that are readily found in a Boricua's kitchen.

Perhaps the greatest beauty in being Puerto Rican is the diversity of our roots, from Southern European, to North and West African, even as far as China; the Puerto Rican culinary diversity is equally as beautiful, taking on aspects of all our ancestors.

The Easy Puerto Rican Pantry

The Puerto Rican pantry is a literal extension of our widely diverse culinary heritage, borrowing ingredients from many points of the globe.

SPICES:

Adobo: Puerto Rican adobo differs from other types. The traditional Puerto Rican version is used to season or dry rub meats, while in Mexico it is used as a marinade. This seasoning, which often blends salt, black pepper, garlic, and oregano, can be found in almost every Puerto Rican kitchen.

Garlic powder: Also common in American cuisine, garlic powder is used to season many Puerto Rican dishes—everything from sauces to stews to seasoning meats for your main course. It's easily found in any supermarket or local store.

Sazón: Another very popular seasoning in the Puerto Rican pantry and one of the more versatile seasonings, typically made up of cilantro, garlic, achiote, and salt. It's available in most supermarkets but is also very easy to make at home.

Cumin: Cumin is a popular seasoning in several cuisines, and Puerto Rican food is no different. This easily attainable spice is the base for many other important seasonings our dishes use.

Oregano: Dried oregano is used in many sauces and stews in Puerto Rican cuisine. You can usually find Mexican or Italian versions of the seasoning in most grocery stores, but the Mexican version is definitely more flavorful and will lend itself to these recipes better. Oregano is a must-have for any spice rack.

DRY GOODS:

Annatto seeds: Although it adds no flavor to meals, annatto seeds are key in making the Achiote Oil that gives Puerto Rican Rice its amazing color. This ingredient can be difficult to find locally, so we order ours online.

Rice: A basic white medium- or long-grain rice is used in Puerto Rico's most popular dish, Arroz con Gandules, as well as many other classic dishes. It is the most important dry good to have stocked in your pantry.

Chicharrónes/Pork Rinds: *Chicharrónes* serve several purposes when cooking; not only are they a snack that can be eaten on their own, but in a recipe like Mofongo they add both texture and flavor to the finished product.

Flour: Flour is a staple of any kitchen or pantry no matter what regional, national, or ethnic cuisine is being prepared. It may well be the most versatile dry good used in cooking. The basic, all-purpose kind will work for these recipes.

Sugar: Used in many recipes, sugar has a special place in the Puerto Rican pantry. For nearly 100 years Puerto Rico was one of the United States' main suppliers of sugar, making the cultivation of it an important part of the island's economy. In these recipes, white granulated sugar works best.

USING DRIED BEANS:

Beans are an integral ingredient in Puerto Rican cuisine. Traditionally, dried beans were used in all these recipes. Today, balancing hectic schedules makes canned beans a very attractive option to save time; just make sure you drain and rinse them thoroughly before using. If you can spare the time, for a taste of authentic Puerto Rican cooking, you can rehydrate dried beans in a few simple steps.

1. Thoroughly rinse the beans under cold running water and remove any remaining debris.
2. Place the beans in a bowl and cover them with fresh cold water.
3. Allow the beans to soak for 12 to 24 hours, then remove from the water and rinse again before using.

CANNED/JARRED GOODS:

Sofrito: Puerto Rican sofrito is culantro/cilantro-based rather than the more typical tomato-based, giving it its distinctive green coloring. It is so often used that sofrito is a must-have at all times.

Gandules Verdes/Pigeon Peas: In many cultures' cuisines, pigeon peas are accompanied by rice. Puerto Rican cuisine took this simple pairing and turned it into its national dish, Arroz con Gandules. Not quite as large or fibrous as kidney or pinto beans, but still nutrient-dense and protein-rich, they turn from green to brown when cooked.

Habichuelas Negras y Rojas/Black Beans and Kidney Beans: Both types of these beans are commonly used in many different meals as ingredients or sides. Inexpensive and easy to store, they have always been a staple of the Puerto Rican diet.

Guava Paste: A thick purée of guava fruit and sugar, this ingredient can be used in both sweet and savory dishes. Served alongside cheese, these two flavors complement each other perfectly. It's typically found in the Goya or Latin American section of the grocery store in a re-sealable tub or onetime-use plastic packet, but it may be difficult to find outside of major urban centers.

Tomato Sauce: This is a typical base ingredient in many sauces regardless of a recipe's origin. So it's not surprising that Puerto Rican food features tomato sauce as well.

Coconut Milk: The abundance of coconuts on the island makes it no wonder that many drinks like Coquito and desserts like Tembleque are made with a milk extracted from the pulp of coconuts.

A note about can sizes: I've included standard US can sizes in ingredient lists, but if your grocery store carries a slightly different size can, one or two ounces more or less won't significantly affect any recipe. For example, coconut milk is generally sold in 13.5-ounce cans, but if you find a 15-ounce can, that's fine to use.

TO CAN OR NOT TO CAN

When I was learning traditional Puerto Rican cooking, I made everything from scratch. I would spend all day on weekends prepping, running from stove, to table, to pantry, soaking beans, and mixing adobo and sazón to ensure I had the right ingredient mix. To save time and make life easier—one of the goals of this book!—I now buy many of the products that used to be made from scratch from a local grocer. I frequently use canned foods when the quality is high enough and, as you may notice thumbing through this cookbook, most Puerto Ricans trust Goya brand products above others due to quality, variety, and availability. The most frequent canned purchases are *habichuelas* (beans) and *gandules* (pigeon peas), and sometimes *habichuelas guisadas* (stewed beans).

OTHER ESSENTIALS

Pique: Pique sauce is a Puerto Rican hot sauce that many restaurants have on all of their tables. It's usually made by steeping hot peppers, seasonings, and fresh herbs in a cider vinegar.

Rum: So popular that this spirit has become synonymous with Puerto Rico itself, it's one of the island's main exports. The main component in many drink recipes, it's also the base to a lot of popular sauces and desserts.

The Easy Puerto Rican Perishables

Just like our spices and dry goods, our perishables are a mixture of well-known favorites and exotic flavors unique to our small tropical island.

REFRIGERATOR AND FREEZER

Cilantro: The main ingredient in Puerto Rico's distinctive version of sofrito that is the base to many of the most popular recipes in the island's cuisine. Fresh cilantro should be in stock at all times.

Codfish: As would be expected for an island, seafood is an important part of Puerto Rico's culinary identity, and none is more widely utilized than codfish. Salted *bacalao* (codfish) is an important start to many stews, salads, and main meals. Be sure to look for fish that is flat white in color without spotting or dark areas. Bone-in fish packs a bit more flavor, but buying deboned fish will save you some stress.

Pork: Pork is such a big part of modern Puerto Rican cuisine that the island's route 184 is known as *La Ruta de Lechón* or "The Pork Highway." You can find many restaurants with pigs roasting on spits along this road in Guavate.

Chicken: Second only to pork in popularity, chicken is eaten in almost every style of Puerto Rican dish. If you venture out of the large urban areas, wild chickens can be seen roaming all over the island.

Beef: While not used as often as the previous three proteins, Puerto Rico has a few amazingly popular dishes made with beef. Foods like Rellenos de Papa utilize beef as part of its amazing filling, *picadillo de carne*.

OTHER FRESH ITEMS

Plantain: A green cooking banana with more sugar and starch than the typical yellow banana found in most peoples' fruit bowls. This is never eaten raw, but once cooked can be used in many forms from a mashed side to fried chips.

Yautía: An important component in Puerto Rican food, this is the root of the elephant ear plant and is used as one of the primary ingredients in the *masa* or dough of Pasteles, a traditional holiday dish on the island.

Cassava: Commonly referred to as yuca, cassava roots are used in Puerto Rican cuisine much the way potatoes are in typical American kitchens. It is a starchy, inexpensive side that can be used in a variety of ways.

Avocado: This widely-loved fruit grows abundantly in Puerto Rico, so it is no wonder it has made its way into the cuisine. Used in many salads, avocados add rich flavor, texture, and important nutrients to our diets.

Potatoes: A basic necessity in nearly every kitchen around the world. A tried-and-true starch that is easy to work with and goes with almost any meal, they should always be on hand because it's a surefire bet you will need them.

IN LIEU OF LARD

A lot of traditional Puerto Rican recipes like Rellenos de Papas and Sorullitos are fried in lard. While frying with lard tastes amazing, it isn't the healthiest way to go. I like to use vegetable or canola oil whether I'm oiling a pan or deep frying a dish. You can also use olive oil for sautéing; just be sure that the oil you choose has a high smoke point, as many of these recipes call for high heat.

Kitchen Essentials for Ease

When my dad first started teaching me to make Puerto Rican food, he went to a small shop and bought me a hand-carved pilon (a wooden mortar and pestle). He wanted me to use the traditional tools to cook with and to have experience with all the tools he used as a kid. This is one of the many measures my dad took to ensure that he passed on his legacy to the future generations.

Oddly enough, it was using the traditional tools and cooking methods that initially intimidated me in the kitchen. I couldn't find some of the specialty ingredients and didn't want to pay the prices for some of the specialized equipment. In time, I found that many of the kitchen essentials I already owned worked just as well as the traditional tools. You don't need to find a Puerto Rican bodega to buy a pilon when you have a perfectly good food processor and access to the Internet. That's the beauty of this cookbook—you don't need expensive tools to make the best authentic Puerto Rican food.

APPLIANCE ADAPTATIONS

There are quite a few Puerto Rican recipes that require you to stand over a pot and tend to them for hours at a time like soups, stews, and the ever popular Pernil. Others require a lot of manual work to make them in the traditional way. However, having friends in the restaurant industry has taught me a lot of little tricks for swapping traditional methods for the ease of modern appliances to create a simpler, more enjoyable experience in the kitchen.

Most of my stews have gone from requiring hours of standing over a large stockpot to using the slow cooker. This doesn't mean you can't make these on the stove top; if that's what you prefer, simply allow all the liquids in the recipe to simmer for a couple of hours over medium heat before starting to add in the other ingredients.

About the Recipes

In this book, you'll find the essential recipes that are important in knowing what Puerto Rican culture and cuisine all are about, as well as recipes that will give you a taste of the varying, modern flavors of island life. My goal is to bring you the most essential and fun recipes to capture Puerto Rico's essence, with simple methods and easy-to-find ingredients. If you know our food already, this will be a great tool to help you make the recipes more easily and often. Conversely, if you have never experienced the culinary delights of the island's cuisine, this is a great introduction to delicious recipes made simple. Either way, the aroma that fills your kitchen from cooking these dishes will be well worth the effort.

THE CHAPTERS

Finding the right recipe can be difficult sometimes when choosing what to cook for that family dinner or get-together. In laying out the chapters in this book I wanted it to be as easy as possible to find the exact type of recipe you may need. Do you have to take the kids to soccer practice after work? Chapter 3 is full of recipes like Churrasco that take 30 minutes or less. Need to put together a quick lunch and drinks for friends to hang out on the deck this afternoon? Chapter 2 has no-cook recipes like a great Tripleta Sandwich and some Mojitos that go together perfectly. Do you plan on making several different recipes from this book and want to prep some bases ahead of time? Check out Chapter 8 with all the staples in Puerto Rican cuisine including Sofrito.

THE TIPS

At the ends of recipes, I offer little notes and tips to help make your life even easier. All these tips will fall into six basic categories:

SUBSTITUTION TIP: When ingredients can be subbed out for flavor, allergens, or alterations.

MAKE-AHEAD TIP: Helpful information on what can be prepped in advance to save time.

LEFTOVER TIP: How to store a dish and for how long, including reheating instructions or tips on repurposing the leftovers into another meal or side dish.

INGREDIENT TIP: Useful information on selecting, preparing, or working with ingredients, plus helpful nutrition facts.

VARIATION TIP: Suggestions for adding or changing ingredients to mix things up a little or try something new with the recipe.

ENTERTAINING/HOLIDAY TIP: Directions for doubling or tripling the recipe to feed more people and/or tips for keeping things warm and pairing with other dishes and wines.

THE INGREDIENTS

Puerto Rican cuisine used to be out of reach to many looking to explore it due to some key ingredients only being available in small shops in Puerto Rican neighborhoods. Over the past 10 years or so, many specialty grocery stores have popped up that cater to Latin Americans, and many big-box grocery stores now feature an International or Latino aisle where these formerly hard-to-find ingredients can now be found easily. Further, the wonder that is the Internet makes getting ahold of once unattainable items as easy as clicking your mouse. What I find most exciting is that many stores in Puerto Rico now accept online orders and ship items right to your door, allowing you to buy authentic products *and* support small, local sellers.

Mojito,
Page 19

2

Beverages and
No-Cook Recipes

JUMPING INTO A BRAND-NEW CUISINE WITH ALL NEW FLAVOR combinations and ingredients can be a little intimidating, which is why I think it's best to begin with the simplest recipes possible. Even if you're familiar with Puerto Rican cuisine, this is a great chapter to start with. And here's the best part—these recipes are all no-cook and no-bake, so we don't even need to head over to the stove to make any of them. Easy drinks, salads, lunches, and desserts that take very little time and effort but yield amazing results, these no-cook recipes will all be winners on the first try.

Piña Colada

MAKES: 4 drinks | **PREP TIME:** 5 minutes

3 cups ice

12 ounces pineapple juice

6 ounces light rum

4 ounces coconut cream

2 ounces dark rum

The perfect recipe to start this short culinary tour of Puerto Rico is one of the most recognizable drinks anywhere. The Piña Colada embodies the dream of living on an island paradise. Originally created in 1963 in San Juan, it became the national drink of Puerto Rico in 1978. This sweet rum-based drink is a favorite the world over, and the best part is that all the ingredients are easily and readily available in any supermarket.

1. Place ice, pineapple juice, light rum, coconut cream, and dark rum into a blender. Blend until completely smooth.

2. Pour into 4 glasses and serve immediately.

   SERVING TIP: Serve in hollowed-out coconuts with a slice of pineapple on the rim of each to feel like you're on the island, wherever you are.

   ENTERTAINING TIP: This recipe is a simple 1 part coconut cream, 2 parts rum, and 3 parts juice. If you're entertaining for a crowd, simply scale up as necessary.

Coquito

Puerto Rican Eggnog

MAKES: 10 drinks | **PREP TIME:** 1 hour (plus 2 to 3 hours chill time)

1 cup dark rum

2 cinnamon sticks

2 (13.5-ounce) cans coconut milk

1 (14-ounce) can condensed milk

½ teaspoon vanilla extract

½ teaspoon ground cinnamon

In Spanish adding "ito/-ita" to the end of the word means "little." If your daughter's name is Rose, you might call her Rosita, meaning "little Rose." Well, that's what *coquito* means—a little coconut. Coquito is a holiday favorite in Puerto Rico, much like eggnog is a holiday favorite in the US. With the sweet flavor of coconut and the smoothness of the rum, it's a simple drink with a new spin.

1. In a jar with a lid add rum and cinnamon sticks. Close and allow to sit for 1 hour.

2. In a blender, add the coconut milk, condensed milk, vanilla extract, and ground cinnamon and purée. Pour in rum and cinnamon stick mixture and shake well to make sure they are combined.

3. Pour everything into a large bottle or pitcher and refrigerate at least 2 to 3 hours. The drink will thicken the longer it rests.

VARIATION TIP: If you like a thinner drink add in about ½ cup water to the ingredients.

STORAGE TIP: The longer Coquito rests, the stronger the flavor gets. You can allow it to rest for up to a month in the refrigerator before serving.

Limón Cocktail

MAKES: 4 drinks | **PREP TIME:** 5 minutes

4 ounces Bacardí Limón

4 ounces coconut rum

2 ounces pineapple juice

Ice

4 lime wedges, for garnish

Puerto Rico has two big rum exporters: Don Q, which is the island's largest rum company, and Bacardí, which is arguably the most famous rum company. Both provide a wide variety of great rums, and this will be the only time you see me picking one over the other for a recipe. This lemon-based cocktail with a hint of sweet pineapple is an easy winner and allows you to experiment with one of the great flavored rums Puerto Rico has to offer.

Combine Bacardi Limón, coconut rum, and pineapple juice in a shaker with ice. Shake well and strain into chilled cocktail glasses. Garnish with a slice of lime and serve.

MAKE-AHEAD TIP: You can make this ahead of time and allow it to chill in a pitcher in the refrigerator.

Cuba Libre

MAKES: 1 drink | **PREP TIME:** 3 minutes

½ lime

Ice cubes

2 ounces light rum

4 ounces cola

When I used to go out for drinks, one of the drinks I ordered all the time was a simple rum and coke. Over the years that evolved into the more sophisticated yet still simple Cuba Libre. This puts a new spin on the classic rum-and-coke cocktail with a hint of lime that balances out the sweetness of the cola. If you can find bottled cola with real sugar cane rather than artificial sweeteners, that really makes the difference. With very few easy-to-find ingredients, you end up with a refreshing Caribbean drink.

Squeeze juice from the lime into a tall glass and add in ice cubes. Pour in the rum and cola, stir well, and enjoy.

ENTERTAINING TIP: This recipe is a simple 2 parts cola, 1 part rum, and the juice of half a lime per glass. Simply scale up that ratio if you're serving a crowd.

INGREDIENT TIP: After juicing the lime, muddle it in the glass, then remove it. Muddled lime makes this drink really pop.

Daiquiri

MAKES: 1 drink | **PREP TIME:** 5 minutes

2 ounces light rum

1 ounce fresh lime juice,
plus 1 lime wedge

1 ounce simple syrup

Ice

Nothing says tropical paradise like a nice chilled drink, and nothing says chilled drink like a daiquiri. This classic cocktail is refreshing, light, and easy to make. Everything you need can be found in any major grocery store. This daquiri is a sweeter drink thanks to the simple syrup, and it goes down easy. Kick back and enjoy.

Combine rum, lime juice, and simple syrup in a shaker with ice. Shake well and strain into a chilled cocktail glass. Garnish with a slice of lime and serve.

ENTERTAINING TIP: This recipe is a simple 2 parts rum, 1 part lime juice, and 1 part simple syrup. Scale up as necessary for entertaining a crowd.

Mojito

MAKES: 1 drink | **PREP TIME:** 5 minutes

12 fresh mint leaves

½ lime cut into 4 slices

2 tablespoons
   granulated sugar

1 cup ice

1½ ounces light rum

½ cup club soda

The mojito is like candy in a glass. This drink just pops and shows how versatile rum can be with the flavor of fresh mint. There is nothing overly complex or complicated about this drink, with no hard-to-find ingredients. Mojitos are an easy addition to any summer day spent relaxing on the patio.

1. Muddle the mint and 1 slice of lime in a glass. Add sugar and 2 more slices of lime and muddle again. (If you don't have a muddler, use the handle of a wooden spoon to crush the ingredients.)

2. Add in ice, and pour rum and club soda over the ice. Stir and serve.

ENTERTAINING TIP: Making a pitcher is very simple. Quadruple the amounts of all the ingredients and add to a pitcher. Refrigerate until you are ready to use.

Yellow Bird Cocktail

MAKES: 1 drink | **PREP TIME:** 5 minutes

½ lime

Ice

1¼ ounces orange juice

1 ounce light rum

1 ounce dark rum

¼ ounce Galliano liqueur

A classic Caribbean cocktail, the Yellow Bird brings to mind beaches, evenings on lounge chairs, and tiki torches. The orange juice gives this fun rum cocktail a nice tropical citrus fruit flavor, but there are many ways to make it—there are probably as many versions of the Yellow Bird as there are places to order them in San Juan. This one is simple and packed with flavor.

1. Juice the lime into a shaker with ice and add the orange juice, light and dark rums, and the Galliano liqueur.

2. Shake well and strain into a tall glass filled with ice.

   VARIATION TIP: Pour 1½ ounces each of light and dark rum into a glass, then add 2 ounces each of a banana liqueur and orange juice.

Guava Margarita

MAKES: 4 drinks | **PREP TIME:** 15 minutes

½ cup fresh lime juice

1 cup tequila

½ cup Grand Marnier

1 cup guava purée

Coarse salt

Guava purée may be an ingredient that you aren't used to seeing in your everyday shopping, but it's easy to find, typically either in the juice or liquor aisles of most stores. If your local chain doesn't carry it, this is an item you can purchase online and not have to worry about spoilage during shipping, as it need not be refrigerated until after it's opened.

1. Mix together lime juice, tequila, Grand Marnier, and guava purée in a large pitcher. Refrigerate until ready to use.

2. To serve, rub a cut lime around the rim of each serving glass, and press the rim into salt. Pour margarita into salt-prepped glass.

Leche de Coco

Coconut Milk

MAKES: 2 to 3 cups | **PREP TIME:** 40 minutes

1 large coconut

2 to 3 cups water

There is almost nothing that says tropical island like a coconut. It is a local, abundant ingredient in Puerto Rico that it is an integral part of the cuisine. Coconuts can be found in any major grocery store. If you have always seen them and just never knew what to make with them, let this be your first recipe using this exotic fruit.

1. Using a screwdriver, pierce one of the eyes in the coconut and tap the end of the screwdriver with a hammer or mallet. Drain the liquid (you can drink it or store it in the refrigerator for up to 4 days).

2. Crack open the coconut using a hammer and break it into small pieces. Carefully run a knife between the shell and the white part of the coconut to remove the meat. If small bits of shell remain on the meat you can use a vegetable peeler to remove them.

3. Place the coconut meat into a blender and pour in water. Make sure there is enough water to cover all the coconut meat. Blend until it is finely grated.

4. Place cheesecloth into a sieve, and place over the container of your choice. Pour the coconut mixture into the cheesecloth and squeeze as much liquid as possible into the container.

5. Refrigerate coconut milk and serve within 3 to 4 days.

INGREDIENT TIP: Bake your coconut for 30 minutes at 350°F. This will soften the coconut meat and make it easier to remove once it has cooled. You can also purchase packaged coconut at many stores and online; simply chop it into small pieces and add it to the blender.

Leche de Arroz

Rice Milk

MAKES: 4 cups | **PREP TIME:** 1 day

1 cup white rice

5½ cups water, divided

1 teaspoon honey

¼ teaspoon vanilla extract

As you'll see in this cookbook, rice is used a lot in Puerto Rican cuisine, even in the drinks. Rice milk is a smooth and sweet drink that's easy to adjust to your own tastes. You'll find there are many versions of rice milk, but this is the easiest way to make it. I use honey to sweeten it, though you can use sugar or even blend in other sweet fruits.

1. Place rinsed rice into a bowl and cover with 1½ cups of water. Allow to soak overnight.

2. Drain the water from rice. Put the rice and the remaining 4 cups of water into a blender and pulse for 1 to 2 minutes. Place a sieve lined with cheesecloth over a bowl and strain the mixture through the cloth. Squeeze the cloth to get as much liquid out as possible.

3. Mix honey and vanilla extract into milk and place into mason jars or a pitcher, allowing it to chill until ready to serve.

STORAGE TIP: Rice milk will keep in the refrigerator for up to 1 week.

Jugo de Carambola

Star Fruit Juice

MAKES: 8 cups | **PREP TIME:** 15 minutes

10 star fruits

4 cups water

½ cup granulated sugar

Ice

Star fruit has a tart flavor with just a hint of sourness. At one point it was somewhat of a specialty item, but most major stores now carry them so you shouldn't have trouble finding them. Star fruit has a refreshing citrus-like juice that goes great with breakfast. Want to feel like you're waking up on our beautiful isle? Make sure to start the day with a glass of star fruit juice.

1. Halve each star fruit and squeeze the ends to push the pulp out of the skin. Place the pulps into a blender.
2. Add the water and sugar and pulse until liquified. Pour through a strainer into a pitcher with ice.

INGREDIENT TIP: A ripe, flavorful star fruit will be yellow to yellow-green in color. If it's more green than yellow, it's not ready to be used yet.

Champola de Guayaba

Guava Smoothie

MAKES: 4 drinks | **PREP TIME:** 10 minutes

---

1 (14-ounce) package guava pulp

1 (12-ounce) can evaporated milk

1 cup water

½ cup granulated sugar

1 teaspoon vanilla extract

Ice

This is a great everyday smoothie with a tropical twist. Guava pulp is another ingredient that is more common and easier to find than you might think, usually found in the juice aisle at the store. Goya is one of my go-to brands that makes a lot of great ingredients throughout this book, including guava pulp.

Place guava pulp, evaporated milk, water, sugar, and vanilla extract in a blender and pulse until liquified. To serve, fill glasses with ice and pour smoothie over ice.

Guava Dip

MAKES: 2 cups | **PREP TIME:** 15 minutes

5 ounces guava paste

2 tablespoons water

8 ounces softened
cream cheese

¼ cup sour cream

2 tablespoons honey

1 minced garlic clove

Salt

Guava and cheese work well together in a lot of recipes, creating a great sweet and savory flavor profile. This guava dip is an easy crossover recipe for those who may be new to Puerto Rican cuisine, and even for those who may not be big fans of Latin food. This dip is a real crowd pleaser, no matter the crowd.

1. Place guava paste and water into a food processor and pulse until smooth. Remove paste and set aside. Rinse out processor.

2. Place the cream cheese, sour cream, honey, garlic, and salt into the food processor and pulse until smooth. Transfer to a serving bowl and fold the guava paste into the cheese mixture.

STORAGE TIP: Tightly cover the dip and store it in the refrigerator for up to 1 week.

Ensalada de Aguacate y Tomate

Avocado and Tomato Salad

MAKES: 4 servings | **PREP TIME:** 15 minutes

FOR THE SALAD

2 large tomatoes, sliced

½ small red onion, sliced

2 avocados, sliced

2 tablespoons chopped cilantro

FOR THE DRESSING

2 limes, juiced

3 tablespoons white vinegar

1 tablespoon olive oil

Salt

Pepper

This simple salad is elevated with the tropical flavors in this recipe. Avocados are bountiful in Puerto Rico and can be found all over the island, and they lend great taste and texture to many dishes. This salad is perfect for a quick meal with lots of flavor.

TO ASSEMBLE THE SALAD

Layer half of the tomatoes, red onion, avocados, and cilantro on a serving plate. Layer in the other half of the ingredients.

TO MAKE THE DRESSING

Whisk together the lime juice, vinegar, olive oil, salt, and pepper in a small bowl, drizzle over the salad, and serve.

Ensalada de Aguacate y Jueyes

Avocado and Crab Salad

MAKES: 4 servings | **PREP TIME:** 25 minutes

1 (8-ounce) can lump
  crab meat

¼ red onion, chopped

½ green pepper, chopped

¼ cucumber, chopped

2 tablespoons
  chopped cilantro

1 lemon, juiced

2 tablespoons olive oil

Salt

Pepper

2 avocados

As is true of any island, seafood is a big part of life in Puerto Rico. There are a number of seafood recipes in this book, but this is a simple one to start out with. This avocado and crab salad is basic in its construction but complex in its flavor. The presentation of it makes it feel like something you would get at a high-end restaurant, even though the ingredients are easy to find and even easier to work with.

1. In a large bowl toss together lump crab meat, onions, peppers, cucumbers, and cilantro. Add half the lemon juice, olive oil, salt, and pepper. Cover and refrigerate until ready to use.

2. Peel and roughly chop the avocados. Drizzle with a little olive oil, salt, and pepper.

3. Spoon some chopped avocado into a lightly greased 1-cup measure and lightly press down, then add some of the crab mixture. Slide the mold off and serve. Add a little more chopped cilantro as garnish if you want.

VARIATION TIP: Add a layer of cooked rice between the avocado and crab layers to make this a more substantial, satisfying meal.

Ensalada de Carambola y Jamón

Star Fruit and Prosciutto Salad

MAKES: 2 servings | **PREP TIME:** 10 minutes

FOR THE SALAD

1 cup lettuce

½ cup arugula

4 ounces prosciutto

1 thinly sliced star fruit

FOR THE DRESSING

1 tablespoon
   sherry vinegar

3 tablespoons olive oil

½ teaspoon garlic powder

Salt

Pork and ham (prosciutto, in this recipe) are big parts of Puerto Rican cuisine; you'll see them in everything from appetizers to main courses and side dishes. A star fruit and ham salad is a delicious, easy pairing that has an extra *wow* factor. This is the perfect salad to serve as an appetizer or pair with a nice summer lunch.

TO ASSEMBLE THE SALAD

1. Rinse, dry, and chop the lettuce. Place lettuce into a medium salad bowl and add the arugula on top.

2. Roughly chop the prosciutto and place it on top of the arugula, then add the thinly sliced star fruit.

TO MAKE THE DRESSING

In a small bowl whisk together vinegar, olive oil, garlic powder, and salt. Drizzle the salad with dressing and serve.

VARIATION TIP: If you don't like prosciutto, sliced serrano ham will work just as well. Add some thinly sliced bell pepper for extra texture and flavor.

Ensalada de Repollo

Cabbage Salad

MAKES: 4 servings | **PREP TIME:** 45 minutes

3 cups sliced cabbage

1½ cups julienned carrots

1 roughly chopped avocado

2 tablespoons olive oil

4 lemons, juiced

Salt

Pepper

Cabbage is a commonly used vegetable in many cuisines worldwide, including Latin and Caribbean. It's an inexpensive and easy-to-find base for this recipe and many others. Cabbage Salad is a nice light and crisp vegetarian start to a full dinner or a light meal on its own—this one works for everything.

1. In a large bowl, mix together cabbage, carrot, and chopped avocado. Add in olive oil and the juice from the lemons.

2. Add salt and pepper to taste, and toss to coat all ingredients evenly. Allow to rest at least 30 minutes to allow flavors to really come through.

VARIATION TIP: Adding a tablespoon of finely chopped cilantro really makes the flavors pop in this salad. If you want to make it a creamy salad you can add ½ cup mayonnaise before tossing it all together.

Ensalada de Pulpo

Octopus Salad

MAKES: 4 servings | **PREP TIME:** 20 minutes

FOR THE SALAD

1 (8-ounce) can
  pre-cooked octopus

½ green pepper, chopped

½ red pepper, chopped

½ red onion, diced

1 small tomato, chopped

FOR THE DRESSING

1 tablespoon olive oil

1 garlic clove, minced

1 tablespoon white vinegar

½ lime, juiced

Salt

I used to make this with fresh octopus and always had a hard time finding it, until one of my friends taught me how to make it with canned octopus instead. Canned octopus is available at most stores now and tastes just as good in this recipe. Worst-case scenario, it's also easy to find online.

TO ASSEMBLE THE SALAD

Drain and rinse the octopus, pat dry, and cut into bite-size pieces. In a large bowl, toss together the octopus, green and red peppers, onions, and tomatoes.

TO MAKE THE DRESSING

In a small bowl whisk together the olive oil, minced garlic, vinegar, lime juice, and salt to taste. Drizzle dressing over salad and toss to coat evenly.

INGREDIENT TIP: If you want to make this with fresh octopus, place it in a pot covered with salted water and bring to a simmer, cover, and allow to cook for about 1 hour. Allow it to cool, then clean and slice before adding to the salad.

Tripleta

Three-Meat Sandwich

MAKES: 1 sandwich | **PREP TIME:** 5 minutes

10-inch French bread loaf

2 tablespoons ketchup

2 tablespoons mayonnaise

4 ounces sliced
  Swiss cheese

4 ounces sliced roast pork

4 ounces sliced
  serrano ham

4 ounces sliced roast beef

¼ cup lettuce, shredded

1 sliced tomato

The Tripleta is an example of one of the amazing street foods Puerto Rico has to offer. Popularized by food trucks in the San Juan area, the name comes from the fact that it is a sandwich of, well, three meats. While it's typically grilled, this is a simpler no-cook version that will please anyone.

1. Slice the French bread loaf in half lengthwise and spread your ketchup and mayo on the inside of the bottom bun.

2. Add the cheese, pork, ham, roast beef, lettuce, and tomato. Close sandwich, slice in half, and serve.

VARIATION TIP: Instead of the roast pork, use shredded Pernil (see page 113), and replace the roast beef with leftover skirt steak from the Jibarito recipe (see page 78). Try it grilled: Place in a panini press until toasted and serve.

Cubano

Cuban Sandwich

MAKES: 4 sandwiches | **PREP TIME:** 20 minutes

1 Cuban bread loaf

4 tablespoons mayonnaise

4 tablespoons yellow mustard

8 ounces sliced Swiss cheese

16 ounces sliced ham

16 ounces sliced roast pork

4 dill pickles, sliced

The Cubano became popular in Puerto Rico in the late 1950s and early 60s when Fidel Castro rose to power in Cuba and Puerto Rico saw an influx of Cuban immigrants. The sandwich brought over by the Cubans, who now called Puerto Rico their home, spread in popularity throughout the island and beyond in Florida, New York, and Chicago, among other places.

1. Cut Cuban loaf into quarters and halve each section lengthwise. Spread the mayonnaise and mustard on the inside of each section.

2. On each sandwich, layer Swiss cheese, ham, pork, and dill pickle slices. Close up and serve.

VARIATION TIP: Place in a sandwich press and toast until warm and the cheese is melted.

SUBSTITUTION TIP: If you can't find Cuban bread, use Italian bread.

Limber de Cheesecake

Cheesecake Popsicle

MAKES: 16 servings | **PREP TIME:** 4 hours

8 ounces cream cheese

1 (14-ounce) can sweetened condensed milk

1 (12-ounce) can evaporated milk

1 cup whole milk

1 teaspoon vanilla extract

1 teaspoon granulated sugar

Despite its name, this dessert typically isn't made as a Popsicle. The traditional way to make these is to put them in small plastic cups and eat them the same way you would eat a push pop. Now I make them using Popsicle molds and sticks, and my kids make less of a mess this way.

1. Place the cream cheese, condensed milk, evaporated milk, whole milk, vanilla extract, and sugar in a blender and blend until smooth.

2. Pour mixture into Popsicle molds or small plastic cups. Place a Popsicle stick into each mold and freeze for at least 4 hours before serving.

Limber de Nutella

Nutella Popsicle

MAKES: 16 servings | **PREP TIME:** 4 hours

---

1 (13-ounce) jar Nutella

1 (14-ounce) can sweetened condensed milk

1 (12-ounce) can evaporated milk

1 cup whole milk

1 teaspoon vanilla extract

1 teaspoon granulated sugar

A simple but tasty variation on the cheesecake Popsicle, these Nutella Popsicles are even quicker and easier. With the rise in popularity of Nutella, this is a more recent addition to Puerto Rican cuisine, and a very welcome one at that.

1. Place the Nutella, condensed milk, evaporated milk, whole milk, vanilla extract, and sugar in a blender and blend until smooth.

2. Pour into Popsicle mold or small plastic cups. Place a Popsicle stick into each and freeze for at least 4 hours before serving.

Churrasco / Skirt Steak,
Page 54

3

30 Minutes or Less

NOW THAT YOU'VE EASED IN TO SOME SIMPLE, NO-COOK Puerto Rican recipes, let's take it a step further. In this chapter we'll explore quick meals that you can make when you're pressed for time or just don't want to spend a lot of time in the kitchen. These recipes range from appetizers to full dinners that will allow you to sample some of Puerto Rico's most popular dishes and fully immerse you in the flavors of the island.

Tostones

Fried Plantains

MAKES: 6 servings | **PREP TIME:** 5 minutes | **COOK TIME:** 15 minutes

3 green plantains

1½ cups olive oil

Salt

Plantains are found in several Puerto Rican dishes. While they may look like unripe, ordinary bananas, they're not, and you don't want to try to substitute them with bananas. Most grocery stores carry plantains now, though the best ones are found at specialty produce markets. For *tostones* you want nice green and stiff plantains—these are underripe and perfect for this recipe.

1. Cut the ends off of each plantain. Find one of the ribs that runs lengthwise and slice along it. Using your fingers or a spoon, remove the skin. Slice the plantains into one-inch medallions.

2. In a sauté pan or skillet, heat enough olive oil to cover the plantains over medium-high heat. Place plantain slices into heated oil and allow to fry for 2 to 3 minutes on each side. Remove the plantains from the frying pan and place on a paper towel to absorb excess oil and cool.

3. Once cool enough to handle, flatten the plantain slices. You can use a tortilla press for this if you have one, or you can use the bottom of a plate, a spatula, or even your hand.

4. Place flattened plantains back into the heated oil and allow to fry until they are a beautiful golden brown, for 3 to 4 minutes. Remove from oil and place on a paper towel to cool. Sprinkle with salt before serving.

Plátanos Maduros

Fried Sweet Plantains

MAKES: 6 servings | **PREP TIME:** 5 minutes | **COOK TIME:** 10 minutes

---

3 ripe sweet plantains

2 cups oil

Salt

While the plantains used for tostones are green, stiff, and underripe, the ones you will want for this recipe should be yellow and spotted. The more dark spots the plantain has, the riper and sweeter it is. Knowing when to cook the plantain completely changes the flavor and texture, and it becomes a brand-new side dish or appetizer.

1. Cut the ends off of each plantain. Find one of the ribs that runs lengthwise and slice along it. Using your fingers or a spoon, remove the skin. Slice the plantain into half-inch sections.

2. Heat oil in a sauté pan or skillet over medium to high heat. When the oil is hot, place the plantains into the pan and cook until they are golden brown, for 2 to 3 minutes per side. Remove from oil and lay on a paper towel to cool.

3. Lightly salt and serve as a snack or with dinner.

VARIATION TIP: For a healthier, no-fry version, bake the sliced plantains at 350°F for 25 minutes until tender.

Puerto Rican-Style Crab Cakes

MAKES: 8 patties | **PREP TIME:** 10 minutes | **COOK TIME:** 10 minutes

2½ tablespoons mayonnaise

2 tablespoons Dijon mustard

1 teaspoon adobo (see page 120)

1 teaspoon sofrito (see page 116)

1 teaspoon minced garlic

½ teaspoon lemon juice

1 beaten egg

1 pound lump crab meat

¾ cup panko bread crumbs

1 tablespoon oil

Crab cakes are a popular dish in many regions, and everyone makes them their own way. Of course, there is a Puerto Rican version of them, too, with some ingredients you may have never used before. Adobo and sofrito are widely used in all Puerto Rican cuisine, and you can find recipes for both in this book. If you don't want to make your own adobo, it can be found in most stores' spice aisles.

1. In a small bowl whisk together mayonnaise, mustard, adobo, sofrito, garlic, lemon juice, and egg.

2. In a medium bowl mix together crab meat and bread crumbs. Fold the mayonnaise mixture into crab mixture, then form 8 patties.

3. In a sauté pan or skillet, heat oil over medium to high heat. Add crab cakes to the pan in batches, avoiding crowding, and cook until they are golden brown, for 4 to 5 minutes per side.

STORAGE TIP: These crab cakes will keep in the refrigerator for 3 to 4 days; any leftovers should be frozen.

Bacalaitos

Codfish Fritters

MAKES: 10 fritters | **PREP TIME:** 5 minutes | **COOK TIME:** 20 minutes

2 cups water

1 pound chopped cod fillet

2 cups flour

1 teaspoon adobo
(see page 120)

1 teaspoon sazón
(see page 121)

½ teaspoon baking powder

½ teaspoon oregano

½ teaspoon cumin

2 tablespoons sofrito
(see page 116)

2 cups oil

Another example of true Puerto Rican street food, *bacalaitos* are a staple of festivals and food trucks that can be found dotted along beaches and in San Juan. They are a savory pancake-like fritter, crispy on the outside and chewy on the inside, which uses one of the most plentiful resources available to people living on an island: fish, a big part of the Puerto Rican diet.

1. Bring 2 cups water to a boil in a saucepan. Place cod into water and boil for 10 minutes.

2. Meanwhile, in a medium bowl whisk together flour, adobo, sazón, baking powder, oregano, and cumin. Once completely combined slowly add in the water and sofrito. You will end up with a thick batter.

3. After 10 minutes, remove the cod from the water, pat dry, and fold it into the batter.

4. Heat oil over a medium to high heat in a sauté pan or skillet. Drop heaping spoonfuls of batter into the pan and cook fritters until golden brown, for 3 to 4 minutes per side.

SUBSTITUTION TIP: You can also use 1 pound frozen salted cod, which can be found at any major grocery store. Soak the fish in a bowl of water for several hours to remove the salt, then rinse. From here the recipe is the same.

Sorullitos de Maíz

Sweet Corn Fritters

MAKES: 15 to 20 fritters | **PREP TIME:** 10 minutes | **COOK TIME:** 10 minutes

2 cups water

½ teaspoon salt

1 tablespoon sugar

1½ cups cornmeal

6 ounces shredded Gouda cheese

2 cups oil

These sweet corn fritters are another Puerto Rican street food, perfect for on-the-go snacks. I like to serve them with a simple dipping sauce of ketchup, mayonnaise, and garlic. Sweet corn fritters have been a staple for decades, and their crispy exterior makes them an irresistible appetizer or side dish.

1. Boil 2 cups water in a medium saucepan. Once at a boil, remove water from heat and stir in the salt, sugar, and cornmeal. Return to heat and cook for 2 to 3 minutes, stirring constantly, until the dough no longer sticks to the pan. Remove from heat and stir in the cheese.

2. Once the dough has cooled enough to handle, scoop out 1 heaping tablespoon at a time and roll into a stick shape.

3. Heat oil over medium to high heat in a sauté pan or skillet (there should be about 2 inches of oil in the pan). Place formed dough sticks into oil and fry until golden brown, for 4 to 5 minutes. Serve as is or with your favorite dipping sauce.

Avena

Puerto Rican Oatmeal

MAKES: 2 servings | **COOK TIME:** 25 minutes

1¾ cups condensed milk

Salt

Sugar

1 tablespoon butter

1 small cinnamon stick

1 cup oats

**Ground cinnamon,
  for garnish**

Breakfast in Puerto Rico isn't that different from breakfast anywhere else in the world, we just have our own little twists on popular classics. A big one is *Avena*, or Puerto Rican oatmeal. Many of the ingredients in this recipe you probably have around the house, so you can easily whip this one together without going to the store.

1. In a medium saucepan, bring condensed milk to a simmer. Add in the salt, sugar, butter, and cinnamon stick. Bring to a full boil, making sure everything except the cinnamon stick is completely combined.

2. Add in oats and turn the heat down, stirring occasionally until oats are cooked to your desired consistency.

3. Remove from the heat and discard the cinnamon stick. Cover the saucepan and allow to rest for 2 to 3 minutes. Garnish with cinnamon before serving.

COOKING TIP: You can make Avena in the microwave by putting all the ingredients in a large microwave-safe bowl and heating at 50 percent power for 5 to 8 minutes.

SUBSTITUTION TIP: You can use regular whole milk in place of condensed milk.

Ensalada de Camarones

Shrimp Salad

MAKES: 6 servings | **PREP TIME:** 10 minutes | **COOK TIME:** 5 minutes

3 tablespoons butter

3 pounds shrimp,
deveined and
tails removed

¼ cup chopped
green pepper

¼ cup chopped red pepper

¼ cup chopped red onion

¼ cup olives

½ lemon, juiced

Salt

Pepper

This shrimp salad is a simple but delicious recipe with common ingredients that are easy to find and work with. On top of that, this is an easy-to-make light meal that will please almost everyone, so it's definitely worth a shot. My father was a big shrimp lover so I ended up making this dish often when he would come over unannounced, leaving me no time to go shopping.

1. Melt butter in a sauté pan or skillet over medium to low heat. Add in shrimp, stirring constantly until shrimp is pink and opaque. Remove shrimp from the pan and allow to cool for several minutes.

2. Toss shrimp, green peppers, red peppers, red onions, olives, and lemon juice in a large bowl, making sure everything gets a nice coating of lemon juice. Season with salt and pepper to taste.

SUBSTITUTION TIP: Use frozen or pre-cooked shrimp to save time. If buying shrimp directly from the freezer case, simply thaw in the refrigerator before tossing with other ingredients. If buying frozen, thaw under cold running water, then pat dry.

Yuca en Escabeche

Pickled Cassava Salad

MAKES: 6 servings | **PREP TIME:** 10 minutes | **COOK TIME:** 20 minutes

1 pound yuca/cassava

Water

⅔ cup olive oil

1 white onion, sliced

3 garlic cloves, minced

3 tablespoons
white vinegar

7 to 8 pimento-stuffed
green olives

Salt

Pepper

Yuca en Escabeche is a perfect pairing with Puerto Rican Pernil (see page 113). Like a great potato salad, this escabeche can accompany almost any dish and will wow everyone. If you've never heard of or worked with yuca, don't worry! It's pretty easy to find and even easier to work with.

1. Peel the skin from twhe yuca and chop it into 1-inch chunks.

2. Bring a large pot of water to a boil. Add in the chopped yuca and boil for 10 to 15 minutes. Drain and rinse the yuca, and set aside.

3. Heat olive oil in a sauté pan or skillet over medium heat. Add in the onions and cook until they soften but before they turn brown, about 5 minutes. Add garlic and vinegar and simmer for another 2 to 3 minutes.

4. Toss the yuca, the mixture from step 3, and the green olives together in a large bowl and let rest for at least 1 hour before serving.

COOKING TIP: Make this recipe a day before you eat it and store in the refrigerator. The flavors will mingle and have more of a pop to them when you serve it.

VARIATION TIP: For a punch of extra flavor, add some capers—a popular addition to this recipe.

Pastelillos de Carne

Meat Turnovers

MAKES: 10 pastelillos | **PREP TIME:** 15 minutes | **COOK TIME:** 10 minutes

3½ cups flour

2½ teaspoons salt

2 teaspoons baking powder

3½ tablespoons vegetable oil

1 lightly beaten egg

¾ cups cold water

1 cup picadillo (see page 123)

2 cups oil

This is one of the first Puerto Rican dishes I ever had at the Puerto Rican festival that's held every summer in Humboldt Park. Street foods like these turnovers were a big part of my childhood and sparked my love for Puerto Rican food. This dish can be made in under 30 minutes if you already have the Picadillo prepared, which I highly recommend as it is a staple in Puerto Rican cuisine and can be used in many dishes.

1. Whisk flour, salt, and baking powder together, combining completely. Slowly whisk in the oil and egg. Add the cold water last and mix until combined.

2. Divide dough into 10 equal pieces. Working on a lightly floured surface, roll out dough into roughly 6-inch circles.

3. Add about 1 tablespoon of picadillo to each. Using your finger, brush the edge of the dough with water, fold over, and press the edges together with a fork.

4. Heat the oil in a sauté pan or skillet over a medium heat (there should be about 2 inches of oil in the pan). When the oil is hot, fry turnovers for 2 to 3 minutes per side, until the dough is golden and flaky. Place turnovers on a paper towel to drain excess oil and cool.

SUBSTITUTION TIP: Goya sells premade dough called discos, which can be used for these turnovers instead of making your own dough.

VARIATION TIP: Picadillo is the traditional filling in these turnovers, but you can use cheese or crab, or any other protein.

Habichuelas Guisadas

Bean Stew

MAKES: 6 servings | **PREP TIME:** 5 minutes | **COOK TIME:** 25 minutes

2 tablespoons sofrito
(see page 116)

1 tablespoon sazón
(see page 121)

1 tablespoon adobo
(see page 120)

1 (8-ounce) can
tomato sauce

½ cup pimento-stuffed
green olives

1 teaspoon alcaparrado
(see page 124)

2 (15-ounce) cans
kidney beans

½ pound potatoes, cubed

Water

Some of the first dishes my dad taught me in Puerto Rican cuisine were different types of stews he would eat when he was a kid. Stews were and are a big part of our cuisine because they're inexpensive to make and serve the whole family, and my dad had a huge family, so they needed a lot of easy recipes to feed everyone. This and Mofongo were my dad's two favorite things to eat.

1. Pour in the sofrito, sazón, adobo, and tomato sauce to a large pot over medium heat. Once it starts to sizzle add in olives and alcaparrado. Allow to simmer for 2 to 3 minutes.

2. Add the beans, potatoes, and 2 cans' worth of water. Turn heat to high, cover, and boil for 20 minutes. Serve over white rice.

VARIATION TIP: Feel free to use any type of beans in place of kidney beans; this versatile recipe will work well with pinto beans, black beans, and chickpeas.

Dairy-Free / Gluten-Free / Nut-Free / Vegan

Yuca con Mojo

Cassava with Garlic Sauce

MAKES: 4 servings | **PREP TIME:** 5 minutes | **COOK TIME:** 25 minutes

1½ pounds yuca, peeled and chopped

Water

1 onion, thinly sliced

¼ cup orange juice

¼ cup lime juice

1 tablespoon chopped cilantro

4 garlic cloves, minced

¼ cup olive oil

½ teaspoon oregano

½ teaspoon cumin

Salt

Pepper

Yuca can be purchased both fresh and frozen. Sometimes it's labeled as tapioca in certain stores. Much like a potato, it's a dietary staple of many Caribbean cultures, especially in Puerto Rico. Yuca con Mojo is a great vegan recipe among the more meat-heavy dishes that are typical in Puerto Rican cuisine.

1. Place 1-inch yuca chunks into a large pot and cover with water. Bring to a boil and cook for 15 to 20 minutes, until the yuca becomes tender. Drain and set aside in a large bowl.

2. In another bowl toss together onions, orange juice, lime juice, cilantro, and garlic. Pour over yuca and set aside.

3. Heat oil in a saucepan over medium to high heat and add oregano, cumin, salt, and pepper. Cook until hot and pour over the yuca mixture.

COOKING TIP: You can cook the yuca ahead of time and reheat it in the microwave if you're in a time crunch.

Arroz al Ajillo con Camarones

Garlic Rice with Shrimp

MAKES: 4 servings | **PREP TIME:** 5 minutes | **COOK TIME:** 20 minutes

½ pound medium shrimp, peeled and deveined

1 teaspoon paprika

Salt

Pepper

¼ cup chopped bacon

4 tablespoons butter

5 garlic cloves, minced

3 green onions, diced

3 cups cooked white rice

An easy and delicious complete dinner, Arroz al Ajillo con Camarones is one Puerto Rican dish that will win anyone over. You might find this in many restaurants in the newer areas of San Juan, where they take classic recipes and add some modern flair to them. Garlic is a theme in island cooking— we use it for just about everything.

1. Place shrimp in a medium bowl and add paprika, salt, and pepper to taste. Toss shrimp so it is evenly coated with seasoning.

2. Cook chopped bacon in a sauté pan or skillet. Once bacon is cooked to the point you like it, add shrimp and cook until pink and opaque. Remove shrimp and bacon from pan but don't drain the fat.

3. Melt butter in the same pan over medium heat, then add garlic and green onion. Once the garlic becomes fragrant add in the cooked rice, stirring so it absorbs the garlic sauce.

4. Add shrimp and bacon back in, stir and cook for 1 to 2 minutes, then serve.

Pollo Frito

Fried Chicken

MAKES: 4 servings | **PREP TIME:** 20 minutes | **COOK TIME:** 5 minutes

2 pounds chicken thighs

3 tablespoons olive oil

1 tablespoon white vinegar

2 garlic cloves, minced

1 teaspoon oregano

Salt

Pepper

1 cup flour

2 cups oil

So far, we've tackled pork, beef, and seafood. Don't worry, I haven't forgotten about chicken! Puerto Ricans use chicken in a lot of our recipes, so we'll start with something that is pretty familiar but with a Puerto Rican twist. Simple fried chicken, packed with the flavor of our little island. Served with Arroz con Gandules (Puerto Rican rice with pigeon peas), you have a plate of Puerto Rican soul food.

1. Rinse and pat chicken dry. Drizzle with olive oil and vinegar, coating chicken on both sides. Add garlic, oregano, salt, and pepper, and rub to make sure chicken is completely coated in seasonings. Cover and set aside for 15 minutes.

2. After 15 minutes, toss chicken in flour.

3. Heat oil in a large pot over high heat. Add flour-coated chicken and fry until golden and crispy, 3 to 5 minutes per side.

COOKING TIP: You can marinate and refrigerate the chicken a day ahead of time. Marinating for a full day will give it great flavor.

Carne Frita

Fried Pork Chunks

MAKES: 8 servings | **PREP TIME:** 20 minutes | **COOK TIME:** 5 minutes

2 pounds pork shoulder

1 tablespoon sazón (see page 121)

1 teaspoon adobo (see page 120)

1 teaspoon oregano

5 garlic cloves, minced

3 tablespoons olive oil

⅓ cup vinegar

2 cups vegetable or canola oil

Another very versatile dish, Carne Frita is a street food that is often eaten at clubs on nights out. These can be served as an appetizer or made with some plantains and rice to make a complete meal. With pork being such a large part of our island cuisine, we find many ways to prep and serve it. Sazón and adobo are the only two ingredients you may not already have, though they can be found at most grocery stores if you don't want to make them.

1. Cut the pork into 1-inch cubes and season with sazón, adobo, oregano, garlic, olive oil, and vinegar, making sure pork is coated evenly. Cover and refrigerate for 20 minutes.

2. Heat about 2 cups of oil in a large sauté pan or skillet over medium heat. Add pork to heated oil and fry for about 5 minutes. Remove from oil and place on paper towels to absorb excess oil, then serve.

Chuletas

Pork Chops

MAKES: 4 servings | **PREP TIME:** 5 minutes | **COOK TIME:** 20 minutes

2 tablespoons olive oil, divided

2 pounds bone-in pork chops

1 tablespoon white vinegar

2 teaspoons adobo (see page 120)

1 teaspoon sazón (see page 121)

½ teaspoon garlic powder

Puerto Rican pork chops are my little brother's single favorite dish to eat. He orders them every time we go to a restaurant, so this was a recipe I had to learn. I came to find that there wasn't much effort required to get the most flavor out of the pork chops. Paired with some Puerto Rican rice, this makes for a quick dinner full of that island feel.

1. Drizzle 1 tablespoon olive oil over pork chops and rub to coat. Season with vinegar, adobo, sazón, and garlic powder, making sure the chops are completely coated.

2. In a sauté pan or skillet heat the remaining tablespoon of oil over medium to high heat. When hot, sear pork chops about 2 minutes on each side. Once they have a nice sear, reduce the heat and cook another 5 minutes on each side.

COOKING TIP: For a stronger flavor, marinate ahead of time. Mix all seasonings with ½ cup olive oil and coat the chops evenly, then refrigerate for 1 to 2 hours before frying.

Arroz Blanco con Carne Bíf

White Rice with Corned Beef

MAKES: 6 servings | **PREP TIME:** 5 minutes | **COOK TIME:** 25 minutes

2 cups water

Pinch salt

1 cup uncooked white rice

1 teaspoon olive oil

2 tablespoons sofrito
   (see page 116)

1 teaspoon oregano

1 tablespoon sazón
   (see page 121)

Pepper

1 (8-ounce) can
   tomato sauce

2 (12-ounce) cans
   corned beef

½ cup corn kernels

1 potato, peeled and diced

Corned beef is a simple and relatively inexpensive main dish that's delicious with a simple rice side. Cooking it with several distinctly Puerto Rican flavors like sofrito and sazón give the beef an extra pop it wouldn't normally have. Other than those two ingredients there isn't much you'll have trouble finding to make this quick and easy dinner.

1. In a small saucepan, boil 2 cups of water with a pinch of salt, then add rice. Cover and simmer for 20 minutes.

2. While the rice cooks, heat olive oil in a large pan over medium heat. Add sofrito, oregano, sazón, pepper, and tomato sauce, cooking for a couple of minutes.

3. Add corned beef. Break apart the beef and cook for a couple of minutes. Mix in the corn kernels and potatoes and cover. Cook for 15 to 20 minutes, stirring occasionally.

4. Divide rice among plates and add corned beef on top of the rice.

SERVING TIP: The Plátanos Maduros (see page 39) are a perfect side to round out this authentic Puerto Rican dinner.

Dairy-Free / Gluten-Free / Nut-Free

Churrasco

Skirt Steak

MAKES: 4 servings | **PREP TIME:** 5 minutes | **COOK TIME:** 12 minutes

1½ pounds skirt steak

½ teaspoon cumin

½ teaspoon ground
  coriander

Salt

Pepper

Churrasco is just as easily served as a main course at a high-end restaurant as it is put on a toasted roll and served at a food truck. It is a versatile meat that is a great representation of Puerto Rican cuisine. It uses a few simple ingredients, most of which you probably already have.

1. Pat the steaks dry. In a small bowl mix cumin, ground coriander, salt, and pepper together and rub the steak with the mixture, coating it evenly.

2. Set oven to broil, and broil steak for about 5 minutes per side. Remove steak from the oven and rest for at least 5 minutes.

3. Thinly slice steaks holding your knife at a roughly 45-degree angle, then serve.

SERVING TIP: Mofongo (see page 68) is the perfect side to have with Churrasco. You can also drizzle a little chimichurri (see page 130) over the steak to give it some punch.

Empanadillas de Guava y Queso

Guava and Cheese Dumplings

MAKES: 10 dumplings | **PREP TIME:** 10 minutes | **COOK TIME:** 10 minutes

3½ cups flour

2½ teaspoons salt

2 teaspoons
 baking powder

3½ tablespoons olive oil

1 lightly beaten egg

¾ cup cold water

10 ounces guava paste

8 ounces cream cheese

Canola or vegetable oil

The sweet and savory flavors of guava and cheese work well together in these fried dumplings. This is a festival and street food that has quickly gained popularity in Puerto Rican homes as a simple dessert. Goya makes a guava paste that is easy to find and works well in a lot of recipes, including this one. You end up with a flaky fried pastry that is the perfect cap to any meal.

1. Whisk flour, salt, and baking powder together. Once completely combined, slowly whisk in the oil and egg. Add in the cold water last and mix until combined.

2. Divide dough into 10 equal pieces. Working on a lightly floured surface, roll out dough into roughly 6-inch circles.

3. Cube the guava paste and cream cheese into ¼-inch chunks. Spoon equal amounts of cheese and guava into the center of each dough circle. Brush a little water around the edge of each disk and fold in half, pressing the edges together with a fork.

4. Heat about 2 inches of oil in a pan over medium heat. Once the oil begins to simmer fry the pastries until they are golden brown, 2 to 3 minutes per side. Let cool on a paper towel and serve.

Yuca Fries with Salsa Rosa,
Pages 65 and 128

4

5 Ingredients or Less

PUERTO RICAN CUISINE CAN SEEM INTIMIDATING BECAUSE of long grocery lists with unrecognizable ingredients. This cookbook is meant to show you that there are plenty of recipes with easy-to-find and uncomplicated ingredients that don't lack anything in the flavor department and are true representations of Puerto Rican culture. In this chapter we will explore the best of simple Puerto Rican cuisine with recipes that use 5 ingredients or less (not counting water, oil, or salt and pepper for seasoning) and will give you a taste of how simple making Puerto Rican food can be.

Funche

Cornmeal Hot Cereal

MAKES: 3 to 4 servings | **COOK TIME:** 20 minutes

3 tablespoons butter

1½ cups milk

1½ cups water

Pinch sugar

Pinch salt

1½ cups cornmeal

Funche is a classic Puerto Rican dish that is derived from Italian polenta, displaying some diversity in Puerto Rico's wide variety of influences. With only a few ingredients that are pretty common in most kitchen pantries, this recipe is an easy win when exploring a new cuisine.

1. In a medium saucepan, melt butter and add milk and water. Stir in sugar and salt to taste and bring the mixture to a boil.

2. Slowly whisk in cornmeal until combined, 2 to 3 minutes. Continue to cook over a medium heat until the funche thickens, then remove from heat and serve.

VARIATION TIP: Funche is usually served one of two ways. The first is as a hot breakfast cereal with some of your favorite sliced fruit on top, or a splash of cream. The other way is to pour it into a large ramekin or a greased pan, then place it in the refrigerator to cool. Once it is cooled and hardened, turn it over onto a serving dish and slice it.

Arepas

Sweet Coconut Cakes

MAKES: 20 cakes | **PREP TIME:** 40 minutes | **COOK TIME:** 10 minutes

2 cups flour

1 teaspoon baking powder

1 cup sugar

Pinch salt

1 cup coconut milk

½ cup vegetable oil

Whether for breakfast, lunch, dinner, or anytime in between, arepas are the perfect snack. They can be sweet or savory depending on how you're feeling, and they go with any meal as a side or appetizer. I have family and friends who use arepas to scoop *guisados* and *asopaos* (stews), like you would use chips.

1. In a medium bowl whisk together flour, baking powder, and sugar until completely combined, and add a pinch of salt to taste. Slowly whisk in coconut milk, stirring until just combined.

2. Lightly flour your hands and knead the dough until it's completely incorporated and becomes sticky. Cover the bowl and allow dough to rest for 30 minutes.

3. Lightly flour a flat surface to work on. Take half the dough and roll it out until it is about ⅛-inch thick. Using a cookie cutter (a 2-inch one will work), cut out your arepas and set aside. Repeat this process with the second half of the dough. You'll have about 20 arepas in total.

4. In a large sauté pan or skillet heat ½ cup vegetable oil. Carefully lower arepas into oil and fry until the edges become a golden color, about 1 minute. Turn arepas and fry another 45 seconds to 1 minute.

5. Transfer arepas to a paper towel to drain excess oil. Serve while they are warm and crisp.

VARIATION TIP: For an even sweeter taste sprinkle a little bit of cinnamon and sugar over the arepas before serving. For a savory arepa, use whole milk instead of coconut milk and only a pinch of sugar, and add in a teaspoon of garlic powder when mixing the dough.

Arañitas

Shredded Plantain Fritters

MAKES: 15 to 20 fritters | **PREP TIME:** 25 minutes | **COOK TIME:** 20 minutes

3 green plantains

Garlic salt

1 cup oil

Arañitas means "little spiders" in Spanish, but don't be put off by the name. These crunchy fried plantains pack a lot of flavor and are a staple in the farms and sugarcane fields of Puerto Rico as a quick savory finger food. In my childhood kitchen, Arañitas were a way to hold over the family until dinner was ready.

1. Cut both ends off of the plantains. Find one of the ribs that runs lengthwise and slice along it. Remove the skin using your fingers or a spoon. Halve the peeled plantains and shred with a cheese grater into a large bowl.

2. Cover the shredded plantains in water and add garlic salt to taste, soaking for 10 minutes (this will allow them to absorb the garlic flavor). Drain the water and place shredded plantains on a paper towel to absorb excess liquid.

3. In a sauté pan or skillet, heat oil over medium to high heat. Scoop 1 heaping tablespoon at a time of the shredded plantains and roll into small balls. Press the balls flat and place them carefully into the heated oil, frying until they are bright yellow, 2 to 3 minutes per side.

4. Remove the arañitas and place onto a paper towel to drain excess oil, then serve.

Puerto Rican Fritters

| **MAKES:** 10 to 15 alcapurrias | **PREP TIME:** 1 hour 30 minutes | **COOK TIME:** 10 minutes |

Salted water

5 green (unripe) bananas

1 pound yautía/taro root

1½ tablespoons achiote oil (see page 117)

Salt

1 pound picadillo, fresh (see page 123) or canned

2 cups oil

Alcapurrias are completely unique to Puerto Rico. My first experience eating them was when I was a kid going to the Puerto Rican Day Parade in Humboldt Park. When my dad was ordering food, I couldn't remember the name of what I wanted and ordered the wrong thing. It was a good thing I did though, because it introduced me to Alcapurrias, and I've been in love with this Puerto Rican street food ever since. This is a dish you can find in any Puerto Rican restaurant on the island or stateside.

1. Fill a large bowl with salted water and peel bananas and yautía. Slice the bananas into roughly 1-inch sections. Chop the yautía likewise into about 1-inch cubes. Place bananas and yautía in the salted water and soak for at least 10 to 15 minutes.

2. Drain the water, then place the small chunks into a food processor and pulse until they are finely diced. Place the mixture in a large bowl and add 1 tablespoon achiote oil, stirring until mixture takes on the color of the oil evenly. Refrigerate your dough mixture for at least 1 hour, and up to overnight.

3. After the dough has rested brush ½ tablespoon of achiote oil on a piece of wax paper. Scoop ¼ cup of the dough onto the wax paper and spread it out into a rough circle with a spoon. Scoop about 1 tablespoon picadillo into the center, then carefully fold the wax paper to bring the edges of the dough together and pinch to seal.

> continued on next page

4. Heat about 2 cups oil in a large sauté pan or skillet over medium to high heat. Using a spoon, carefully place alcapurrias into the heated oil and fry until golden, 2 to 3 minutes per side. Remove from oil and place on paper towels to drain excess oil. Serve warm, with a side of pique (see page 126).

VARIATION TIPS: My dad put his own spin on this recipe; instead of achiote oil, he would use about 1 tablespoon of sazón to add coloring to the masa (dough) mixture. While I have only made my alcapurrias with picadillo, my brother makes his with many different fillings, like shrimp or chicken. Get creative with your fillings!

MAKE-AHEAD TIP: You can easily make these a few days ahead of time. Complete steps 1 through 3, then refrigerate for up to 3 days.

Rellenos de Papa

Stuffed Potatoes

MAKES: 10 servings | **PREP TIME:** 15 minutes | **COOK TIME:** 40 minutes

2 pounds potatoes

Water

Salt

4 tablespoons butter

1 egg

½ cup cornstarch

1 pound picadillo, fresh
(see page 123) or canned

2 cups oil

I once tried Alcapurrias because I ordered the wrong food by mistake. Well, what I was actually looking for, but didn't know the name of as a little kid, was rellenos de papa, maybe the most popular Puerto Rican street food. My son has inherited my love for them, so much so that when we went to Puerto Rico last spring, he was determined to try an authentic one made on the island. This recipe is one of my personal favorites.

1. Peel and cut potatoes into about 1-inch cubes, then place them in a large pot with enough water to cover potatoes. Add a little salt to the water, and boil potatoes about 20 minutes until they are soft and fork tender.

2. Drain the water and place potatoes in a large bowl with the butter, egg, salt to taste, and 1 tablespoon cornstarch. Mash ingredients together; they will be a little thicker and dryer than regular mashed potatoes. Let cool enough to be handled with your bare hands.

3. Divide the potatoes into 10 equal portions. Lightly coat your hands with flour and roll the potatoes into balls. Create an indent in the center of each and spoon in about 1 tablespoon of picadillo. Close up the potato around the meat and roll the ball in the remaining cornstarch.

4. Heat 2 cups of oil in a sauté pan o# skillet over medium heat. Place the balls into the heated oil and fry until golden on all sides, 1 to 2 minutes. Remove from skillet and place on paper towels to drain excess oil and cool.

SUBSTITUTION TIP: You can easily make this recipe with instant mashed potatoes. Follow the instructions on the package and add adobo to taste to season the potatoes. Remember, you want the potatoes to be thick and dry to work with, so use slightly less liquid than what the package instructions call for.

Dairy-Free / Gluten-Free / Nut-Free / Vegan

Casabe

Cassava Bread

MAKES: 5 flatbreads | **PREP TIME:** 15 minutes | **COOK TIME:** 15 minutes

1 pound yuca (cassava root)

Salt

Casabe is a simple flatbread that is enjoyed across the Caribbean and is perfect with almost any meal or to eat on its own. The versatility of casabe is well known; you can enjoy it hot and fresh right after it's made, or enjoy it later as a midnight snack. One of the only ways my brother eats it is with a spread of strawberry preserves and a glass of milk.

1. Peel and grate the yuca using the finest grate. Place finely grated yuca into a cheesecloth and squeeze excess moisture into a bowl. You want to remove as much liquid as possible.

2. Place grated yuca into a bowl and add a pinch of salt. Break apart the yuca, making sure there are no clumps, and divide into 5 equal portions.

3. Heat a skillet over low to medium heat. Once the pan is hot, place one portion of grated yuca in the center of the pan, using a spatula to spread it out. Cook until golden, 2 to 3 minutes, then flip and cook the other side until golden. Repeat with the other portions.

SERVING TIP: You can serve Casabe warm when it's soft and pliable, or allow it to cool and it will harden and have a cracker-like consistency.

Yuca Frita

Yuca Fries

MAKES: 4 servings | **PREP TIME:** 5 minutes | **COOK TIME:** 25 minutes

3 pounds yuca

Water

3 cups canola oil

Salt

Yuca fries, yuca frita, or sometimes affectionately called fried yuquitas, are a prime example of the fried tuber that exists in nearly every culture but made here distinctly Puerto Rican. My aunt would make yuca frita when she had guests who weren't overly familiar with Puerto Rican cuisine. As with most side dishes in this cookbook, this is very easy to make and goes with almost everything. Give this a try sometime with a cheeseburger in place of French fries.

1. Peel your yuca and cut into about 4-inch-long sticks. (I prefer mine closer to a steak fry, but some people like them thinner).

2. Place in a pot with enough water to cover the yuca by 1 inch. Bring to a boil and simmer for about 20 minutes, or until the yuca is soft yet still firm enough to hold its shape.

3. Drain the water. In a sauté pan or skillet heat the oil over medium heat. Once the oil is hot, place the yuca in the skillet and fry until golden brown, 2 to 3 minutes.

4. Place cooked yuca on paper towels to drain the excess oil and serve with Salsa Rosa (see page 128).

Arroz Amarillo

Yellow Rice

MAKES: 6 servings | **COOK TIME:** 30 minutes

4 tablespoons achiote oil, fresh (see page 117) or purchased

2½ cups rice

4½ cups chicken stock

2 teaspoons sazón

Salt

Besides plain white rice this is probably the simplest Puerto Rican rice recipe, and that is saying a lot for an island that has more ways to cook rice than square feet of land. This basic *arroz amarillo* is a good way to dip your toes into Puerto Rican cuisine.

1. Heat the oil in a large pot over medium heat. Add rice and cook for a couple of minutes stirring occasionally.

2. Pour in the chicken stock, sazón, and salt. You want enough chicken stock to cover all of the rice by 1 inch. Cover and bring to a boil, then reduce heat to low and cook, covered, for another 20 minutes. If the rice is undercooked once all the stock is absorbed, add in a little water, cover, and continue to cook on low until rice achieves desired consistency.

Pulled Pork Sliders

MAKES: 4 servings | **PREP TIME:** 10 minutes | **COOK TIME:** 15 minutes

2 green plantains

6 tablespoons oil

1 cup coconut milk

½ teaspoon chipotle chili pepper spice (McCormick makes a good one)

¼ cup cilantro

Salt

3 cups pulled pork, canned

I ate these for the first time in a small restaurant in Isla Verde on our most recent trip to Puerto Rico. While this is a newer recipe to me, I quickly fell in love with it. This puts a Puerto Rican twist on a classic American pulled pork slider.

1. Score the plantain lengthwise along one of the ridges, and remove the peel. Slice into 1-inch pieces.

2. Heat about 4 tablespoons of oil in a sauté pan or skillet. Fry plantains until they start to brown, roughly 2 minutes. Flip and fry for another 2 minutes, then remove from heat and place on a paper towel.

3. Once they're cool enough to handle, smash plantains on a piece of wax paper using the bottom side of a plate to flatten them.

4. Heat another 2 tablespoons of oil in the skillet and fry plantains again for 2 minutes per side. Remove plantains and place on paper towels to drain excess oil.

5. Put coconut milk, chipotle pepper chili spice, cilantro, and salt in a food processor and pulse until smooth and well combined.

6. Build sliders with shredded pork in between 2 fried plantains. Drizzle each with the chipotle sauce and serve.

SUBSTITUTION TIP: Use leftover Pernil (see page 113) for an even tastier Puerto Rican dish.

Mofongo

Mashed Plantains

MAKES: 4 servings | **PREP TIME:** 10 minutes | **COOK TIME:** 10 minutes

2 garlic cloves

1 cup plus 1 tablespoon olive oil

Salt

3 green plantains

1 cup chicharrónes, homemade (see page 118) or purchased

A few of the recipes in this chapter are family favorites in my house. When my dad used to come over no other dish would put a smile on his face like mofongo. While I love mofongo with steak or even lobster, my dad would have it with a simple side of rice and some beans. He said that's how his mom used to make it all the time when he was a kid, and he still enjoyed it the same way.

1. Put garlic in a large pilon. Add 1 tablespoon olive oil and salt, and mash until you get an oily paste. Set aside.

2. Cut both ends off of the plantains. Find one of the ribs that runs lengthwise and slice along it. Peel the skin off using your fingers or a spoon and slice the plantains into 1-inch pieces.

3. Heat 1 cup olive oil over medium to high heat (use enough to cover the sliced plantains in the bottom of the pan). Fry plantains for 2 to 3 minutes per side. Remove from oil and place on a paper towel to cool.

4. Add fried plantains and chicharrónes to the pilon and mash together. Once completely combined, scoop out and serve.

VARIATION TIP: Mofongo can be served as a main course with a side of white rice. I have often had it as a side dish drizzled with an Ajillo sauce and plated with Churrasco. You can also roll it into small dumpling-like balls and serve in soup. Feel free to use store-bought pork rinds in place of the chicharrónes to save time.

COOKING TIP: While traditionally made in a pilon, most restaurants now use food processors to make Mofongo. This is a perfectly acceptable way to prep this meal and will save you some time and effort.

Piononos de Carne

Meat-Stuffed Sweet Plantains

MAKES: 12 pinwheels | **PREP TIME:** 10 minutes | **COOK TIME:** 15 minutes

3 ripe yellow plantains

1 cup vegetable oil

1 cup picadillo, fresh (see page 123) or canned

2 eggs

Pinch salt

Piononos are a cool mix of sweet and savory flavors. They exist in several different cultures, but they usually take the form of pastries. Of course, in Puerto Rico we have to do things a little bit differently. Instead of making a pastry, we use the sweet plantains that are plentiful on the island to make pinwheels, which are then stuffed with savory picadillo.

1. Cut both ends off of the plantains. Find one of the ribs that runs lengthwise and slice along it. Peel the skin off using your fingers or a spoon. Slice lengthwise; you should have 4 to 5 slices per plantain.

2. Heat the oil in a large sauté pan or skillet over medium to high heat. Once the oil begins to sizzle, lay the plantain strips in the skillet and fry for 3 to 4 minutes per side. Remove from oil and roll into small pinwheels, placing toothpicks in the ends so they hold the circular shape. Make sure there is a small hole in the middle for the picadillo filling.

3. Spoon picadillo into the center of each pinwheel.

4. In a small shallow dish beat the eggs with a pinch of salt. Dip the filled pinwheels into the egg and place back in the oil, frying for 3 to 4 minutes. Place pinwheels on paper towels to drain excess oil and let cool before serving.

VARIATION TIP: Add shredded cheese on top of each pinwheel before frying them the second time, letting the cheese melt before serving. I love my picadillo, so I tend to stuff everything with it, but feel free to experiment with different fillings like crab or lobster. This recipe will work with almost any filling and be delicious.

Pinchos de Pollo

BBQ Chicken Kabobs

MAKES: 8 servings | **PREP TIME:** 2 hours | **COOK TIME:** 10 minutes

4 pounds chicken thighs

1 tablespoon adobo, fresh (see page 120) or purchased

1½ tablespoons sazón, fresh (see page 121) or purchased

2 teaspoons oregano

1 tablespoon olive oil

⅓ cup barbecue sauce

This may be one of the most popular recipes on my You-Tube channel and Facebook page. The sheer simplicity makes it a favorite for just about everyone who comes across it. Barbecuing chicken on the grill is a universally loved way to cook it, no matter where you're from. Add in the amazing Caribbean flavors of this Puerto Rican version, and it's easy to see why this one is a winner.

1. Cut chicken thighs into about 1-inch cubes, and put in a large bowl. Add adobo, sazón, oregano, and olive oil to the chicken. Toss until the chicken is completely coated. Cover the bowl and marinate in the refrigerator for at least 2 hours.

2. After the chicken has marinated, remove from the refrigerator. Heat the grill while you place the chicken onto skewers. Lay skewers on the grill and cook until chicken reaches an internal temperature of 165°F. Brush with your favorite barbecue sauce and serve.

VARIATION TIP: I often make pork shoulder kabobs on the grill using a different marinade: 1 tablespoon oregano, 1 teaspoon cumin, 5 minced garlic cloves, ½ cup brown sugar, ⅓ cup orange juice, 2 tablespoons lime juice, and 1 tablespoon light rum. Marinate cubed pork in the refrigerator for at least 2 hours; the rest of the recipe is the same.

Milanesa de Res

Breaded Steak

MAKES: 6 servings | **PREP TIME:** 10 minutes | **COOK TIME:** 15 minutes

3 cups panko
  bread crumbs

2 tablespoons salt

2 tablespoons pepper

1 tablespoon adobo,
  fresh (see page 120)
  or purchased

1 teaspoon garlic powder

2 eggs

6 thinly sliced steaks
  (I use top round)

Oil

While I am a fan of the Jibarito on page 78, my little brother prefers this breaded steak sandwich. This is one recipe my dad used to make all the time for us, and we always felt like we were getting a special treat. At the time we didn't know that Dad was making the same thing for himself, just putting ours on a bun while he ate his steak with rice. When I told my little brother that Dad was teaching me to cook, this is the first meal he asked me to make.

1. In a shallow dish whisk together panko bread crumbs, salt, pepper, adobo, and garlic powder. In a second shallow dish beat the eggs.

2. Take each steak and press both sides into the bread crumb mixture, then dip in beaten eggs, and back through the bread crumbs a second time. Set aside on a plate.

3. Add about ½ inch of oil into a large sauté pan or skillet and heat over medium to high heat. Once the oil is hot, add the breaded steaks and fry until the breading turns a nice golden brown, 2 to 3 minutes per side. Remove from the skillet, place on paper towels to drain excess oil, and serve.

VARIATION TIP: These steaks can be served as the main dish with a side of rice and beans or served as a sandwich on a toasted bun with some French fries.

Flan

Caramel Custard

MAKES: 6 servings | **PREP TIME:** 8 minutes | **COOK TIME:** 35 minutes plus 1 hour chill time

---

1¼ cups granulated sugar, divided

Water

1 (12-ounce) can evaporated milk

5 eggs

⅛ teaspoon salt

1 teaspoon vanilla

Flan is probably the most traditional of all Puerto Rican desserts. My brother and I had eaten it hundreds of times, but we always feared it would be too complicated to try to make it ourselves. When I finally decided to tackle learning it, I was pleasantly surprised at how easy it really is to make.

1. Pour ¾ cup sugar and ¼ cup of water into a microwave-safe glass bowl, and stir until the sugar is completely dissolved. Microwave until mixture becomes a golden honey color, 5 to 6 minutes. Watch carefully so as not to let it burn.

2. Pour caramel into ramekins and set them in a deep baking dish.

3. Whisk together the evaporated milk, eggs, salt, vanilla, and ½ cup of sugar, and divide this mixture evenly among the prepared ramekins.

4. Pour water into baking dish about halfway up the ramekins. Bake at 325°F until the flan is set, 20 to 25 minutes. Using tongs or an oven mitt, remove ramekins from baking dish and place in the refrigerator to allow to cool completely, at least 1 hour.

5. Once cooled, gently run a butter knife between the edge of the ramekin and the flan. Turn the ramekin upside down and slide the flan onto a plate to serve.

COOKING TIP: My brother doesn't like to bake so he microwaves his flan. To do this, complete steps 1 through 3, and then microwave the flan-filled ramekins on high for about 8 minutes with a serving plate over top so they don't overflow. Then cool in the refrigerator as above.

VARIATION TIP: You can use 1 (13.5-ounce) can of coconut milk instead of evaporated milk to make Flan de Coco (coconut flan). Top it with a little whipped cream, fruit, or ice cream.

Tembleque

Coconut Custard

MAKES: 6 servings | **PREP TIME:** 2 minutes | **COOK TIME:** 8 minutes plus 2 hours chill time

2 (13.5-ounce) cans coconut milk

½ cup cornstarch

½ cup sugar

¼ teaspoon salt

Water

Cinnamon

My dad and I spent a lot of time together while he was teaching me how to make Puerto Rican dishes. The first time I made *tembleque* was one of the funniest afternoons we spent together. He had me cracking up as he explained how the name of this dessert means "jiggly"—and how he would often get in trouble with my mom for calling her tembleque.

1. Pour coconut milk into a large saucepan. Whisk in cornstarch until mixture is smooth, then add the sugar and salt.

2. Heat the coconut milk mixture over medium heat, stirring constantly until the mixture begins to thicken, then remove custard from heat.

3. Sprinkle the insides of 6 ramekins with a little cold water, then spoon the custard evenly into the ramekins. (The water helps to keep the custard from sticking to the ramekins.) Cool the custard to room temperature, then place ramekins in the refrigerator to chill for 2 hours.

4. Run a butter knife around the edges of the ramekins to loosen custard, then turn it upside down and slide it onto a plate. Top with cinnamon to taste and serve.

Camarones Guisados Criollos / Creole Shrimp Stew,
Page 84

5

One-Pot Recipes

FAMILY IS VERY IMPORTANT TO PUERTO RICANS, AND THIS comes across in the meals we eat. Dinner is a time for families to gather together at the end of the day, break bread, and share their experiences. For this reason, one-pot recipes are a huge part of our cuisine and culture—meals that make it easy and inexpensive to feed a lot of people without too much work. In this chapter we will explore some great one-pot and one-skillet recipes that are simple to create and great for feeding the whole family.

Bolitas de Yuca

Cheesy Yuca Balls

MAKES: 20 bolitas | **PREP TIME:** 5 minutes | **COOK TIME:** 35 minutes

Water

Salt

1 pound frozen yuca

6 ounces cheddar cheese, cubed

Pepper

2 cups oil

This recipe is made in both a pot and a skillet so technically it's a two-pot dish, but it's a great introduction to this chapter as these *Bolitas* are the perfect little appetizer for the one-pot dinners to follow. They are the Caribbean equivalent to mozzarella sticks (except these are way better) and they complete the look, feel, and mood of any Puerto Rican get-together.

1. Fill a large pot with water. Add about 1 tablespoon of salt and bring to a boil.

2. Place yuca into boiling water and cook until fork tender, 20 to 25 minutes.

3. Drain the water from the yuca and remove the wood stems. Season cores with salt and pepper and mash until they are the consistency of mashed potatoes.

4. Take 1 tablespoon at a time of the mashed yuca and place one of the cheese cubes into the center, closing the yuca around the cheese. Repeat with the rest of the yuca.

5. Heat about 2 cups of oil in a sauté pan or skillet over medium heat. Add the yuca balls and fry until golden brown, 1 to 2 minutes per side. Remove from the skillet and place on paper towels to drain excess oil.

VARIATION TIP: I enjoy the sharp taste of cheddar cheese in these bolitas, but my little brother prefers mozzarella cheese—both work great, and mozzarella melts quicker, making the bolitas a little cheesier.

ENTERTAINING TIP: These bolitas are great on their own, but they're even better with Salsa Rosa (see page 128). You can also make a sweet and savory guava dipping sauce by mixing 2 tablespoons of guava paste with ¼ cup white vinegar; microwave until the paste is completely melted into the vinegar, stir, and serve.

Guanimes

Corn Dumplings

MAKES: 8 servings | **PREP TIME:** 15 minutes | **COOK TIME:** 1 hour

2 cups corn flour

¼ teaspoon ground anise

1 cup coconut milk

½ cup honey

Banana leaves for cooking
(see page 131 for prep)

Salted water

Guanimes are the perfect side dish for Puerto Rican stews. Later in this chapter I have a recipe for *Bacalao Guisado*, a codfish stew for which these corn dumplings are a great accompaniment. These dumplings are famously paired with this stew to provide perfect balance—think of a grilled cheese sandwich with warm tomato bisque on a chilly fall day. But guanimes aren't just for stews; they are wonderful on their own as well.

1. In a medium bowl combine corn flour, ground anise, coconut milk, and honey and mix until smooth.

2. Cut the banana leaves into roughly 8-by-8-inch squares. Spoon about 2 tablespoons of the corn flour mixture into the center of each leaf. Roll the leaf like a cigar; there should be about 1½ inches on each end of the leaf that has no corn mixture in it. Pinch and roll the ends to seal them, and tie with cooking twine.

3. Fill a large pot with salted water (use no more than ½ teaspoon salt) and bring to a boil, then reduce the heat to a gentle simmer. Place the rolled banana leaves into the water and simmer for 1 hour.

4. Unwrap leaves and serve.

INGREDIENT TIP: I purchase my banana leaves from a local produce store, but Goya sells pre-packaged, ready-to-use banana leaves if you'd prefer to skip the prep step.

SUBSTITUTION TIP: If you can't find ground anise in your spice aisle, look for ground fennel, which has a very similar flavor profile; while not exactly the same, it will work in this recipe in the small amount needed.

Jibarito

Puerto Rican Steak Sandwich

MAKES: 2 sandwiches | **PREP TIME:** 35 minutes | **COOK TIME:** 25 minutes

1 tablespoon sazón
(see page 121)

1 teaspoon adobo
(see page 120)

1½ teaspoon garlic
powder, divided

1 tablespoon olive oil

1 teaspoon white vinegar

½ pound skirt steak

2 green plantains

¼ cup mayonnaise

¼ cup ketchup

Shredded lettuce

Sliced tomato

In my house, a tradition is that on your birthday you get to pick a restaurant and choose whatever you want to eat. Every year my son picks a small Puerto Rican restaurant by our house and orders a *Jibarito*. While it doesn't originate from the island itself, the jibarito was created by Puerto Rican chef Juan Figueroa at his restaurant, Borinquen, in Humboldt Park back in the mid-1990s. The Jibarito has become a wildly popular sandwich for stateside Puerto Ricans no matter where they live.

1. In a large bowl whisk together sazón, adobo, 1 teaspoon of garlic powder, olive oil, and vinegar.

2. Trim the fat from the skirt steak and place in the bowl, completely coating it with the marinade. Cover the bowl and allow steak to marinate for at least 20 minutes.

3. Cut both ends off of the plantains. Find one of the ribs that runs lengthwise and slice along it. Peel the skin off using your fingers or a spoon. Slice in half lengthwise.

4. Heat oil in a large sauté pan or skillet over medium heat, then fry plantain strips for 3 to 4 minutes per side. Remove from oil; while still warm, smash the plantains so you end up with long, wide, flat strips. Place back in the oil and fry for another 2 to 3 minutes per side, then place them on paper towels to drain excess oil.

5. Drain all but 2 tablespoons of oil from your skillet and return to medium heat. Sear steaks 2 to 3 minutes per side, then remove from skillet and let rest for about 5 minutes.

6. While steak is resting mix together mayonnaise, ketchup, and ½ teaspoon garlic powder in a small bowl.

7. To assemble the sandwich, brush mayonnaise mixture on 1 slice of fried plantain. Then layer your steak, lettuce, and tomato, and another fried plantain. Slice in half like a sub and serve with a side of rice.

VARIATION TIP: Add a slice of mozzarella or your favorite cheese to the jibarito to make it even more mouth-watering.

Arroz con Gandules

Puerto Rican Rice with Pigeon Peas

MAKES: 6 servings | **COOK TIME:** 40 minutes

¼ cup achiote oil
(see page 117)

1 cup sofrito (see page 116)

Salt

Pepper

2 cups white rice

2 (15-ounce) cans *gan-dules verdes* (green pigeon peas)

4 cups water

3 packets Goya chicken bouillon

You haven't really eaten rice until you have tried this Puerto Rican national dish. *Arroz con Gandules* made me want to learn Puerto Rican cuisine from my dad. Just like I did, many people fall in love with our food once they try this rice, and it is easily the most popular recipe on my YouTube channel. There are as many variations to it as there are families on the island, as Arroz con Gandules is not only one of the most popular dishes but also one of the most versatile, often used as a side to another great entrée or as a main course on its own.

1. Heat oil in a *caldero* or Dutch oven over high heat until the oil starts to sizzle. Add the sofrito, salt, and pepper and cook, stirring often for about 5 minutes.

2. Stir in rice making sure it is evenly coated. Cook for a couple of minutes, then add pigeon peas, water, and chicken bouillon.

3. Bring mixture to a boil without stirring. Once boiling, stir, lower the heat, then cover and simmer for about 20 minutes.

4. Stir rice and serve.

VARIATION TIP: A lot of people add ham or bacon to this dish. If using, add about ½ pound at the same time as the sofrito. You can also add 2 tablespoons chopped pimento olives with the pigeon peas for an extra kick.

Arroz con Pollo

Rice with Chicken

MAKES: 6 servings | **PREP TIME:** 5 minutes | **COOK TIME:** 1 hour 5 minutes

---

2 tablespoons olive oil

2 pounds chicken thighs

½ cup diced onion

¼ cup chopped green olives

½ cup sofrito (see page 116)

2 tablespoons capers

1 (12-ounce) can tomato sauce

2 cups white rice, uncooked

4 cups water

Arroz con Pollo is a widely popular Puerto Rican meal. It shows off our love for the one-pot dishes that allow the flavors of all the ingredients involved time to cook and really meld together. You can walk into any Puerto Rican restaurant whether on the island or stateside and order this straight off the menu. Arroz con Pollo will quickly become a go-to recipe in any home.

1. Heat oil in a *caldero* or Dutch oven over high heat. Place chicken thighs into heated oil and cook for 4 to 5 minutes per side, just enough to brown the chicken but not cook all the way through. Remove chicken from caldero and set aside.

2. In the caldero, add diced onions and cook until they soften and start to become translucent, about 5 minutes. Add olives, sofrito, capers, and tomato sauce; mix together and cook for another 5 minutes.

3. Reduce heat to low and add in the rice and water, then place the chicken back in. Simmer for 20 minutes, stir, then cover, simmering for another 25 minutes.

COOKING TIP: You might feel the need to stir the rice as it cooks. Resist this urge! Stirring your rice while it cooks will make it too sticky.

VARIATION TIP: Traditionally this was made with bone-in chicken thighs, which is how my dad and his family cooked it. I have always used boneless thighs. If you use bone-in, they should be tender enough by the time they finish cooking to easily pull the meat away from the bone with a fork.

Arroz con Salchichas

Rice with Sausage

MAKES: 6 servings | **PREP TIME:** 10 minutes | **COOK TIME:** 50 minutes

3 tablespoons sofrito
(see page 116)

2 teaspoons sazón
(see page 121)

2 (5-ounce) cans
Vienna sausage

2 (8-ounce) cans
tomato sauce

Salt

¼ cup olive oil

3 teaspoons
alcaparras (capers)

2 cups white rice

1¾ cups water

You might be noticing a pattern: We Puerto Ricans love our rice. Simple rice recipes are great for feeding the whole family without spending a lot of money or trying to create overly complex meals. Rice is such an essential part not only of Puerto Rican cuisine but the island's culture as well; each recipe is a little different depending on what it's served with.

1. Add sofrito, sazón, sausages plus their liquid from the cans, tomato sauce, salt, oil, and *alcaparras* to a large caldero or Dutch oven. Bring to a simmer over low heat, then add in rice and simmer for another 5 minutes.

2. Pour the water into the caldero. Bring to a boil, then stir, scraping the rice from the bottom of the pot to prevent burning. Cover the pot and reduce the heat to low and simmer for about 20 minutes.

3. Uncover and stir rice again, making sure no rice is sticking to the bottom, recover, and cook for another 10 minutes. Remove from heat and let rest, covered, for 5 minutes before serving.

VARIATION TIP: I have a few friends who also like to put kidney beans in this dish. Try serving your Arroz con Salchichas with the Plátanos Maduros (see page 39).

Carne Mechada

Pot Roast

MAKES: 8 servings | **PREP TIME:** 15 minutes | **COOK TIME:** 2 hours 30 minutes

---

4½ tablespoons
olive oil, divided

2 tablespoons white
wine vinegar

1½ tablespoons adobo
(see page 120)

1 teaspoon oregano

3 pounds round or
chuck roast

1 cup cubed ham

⅓ teaspoon garlic powder

3 chopped onions

1 cup cooking sherry

2 cups water

Salt

Pepper

2 chopped carrots

2 potatoes, peeled
and chopped

Puerto Rican pot roast is a little bit different than other versions in several ways. Not only is this one made on the stove top rather than roasted in the oven, we also stuff it with even more great ingredients. Carne mechada takes a little bit of time to make but is not overly complex (thanks to one pot!) and comes out tasting amazing.

1. Combine 2 tablespoons olive oil, 2 tablespoons vinegar, 1 tablespoon adobo, and oregano in a small bowl.

2. Using a long knife make a slice in the center of your roast. Place the roast in a large bowl or baking dish and coat evenly with the marinade. Rest for at least 15 minutes.

3. In a large caldero or Dutch oven, heat ½ tablespoon oil over medium heat. Add in ham, garlic powder, ½ tablespoon adobo, and onions, and sauté about 5 minutes. Remove sautéed ingredients from pot, and stuff them into the slit you made in the roast.

4. Heat 2 more tablespoons oil in your caldero over medium heat. Place roast in heated oil and sear on all sides. Pour sherry and water into the pot and season with salt and pepper to taste. Cook, uncovered, until the liquid starts to steam, then turn down to low heat, cover the pot, and simmer for about 2 hours, checking the liquid levels often. Add water if needed. With about 25 minutes left, mix in the carrots and potatoes, then serve.

SERVING TIP: Arroz Amarillo (see page 66) is the perfect side for this dinner.

VARIATION TIP: You can replace the cubed ham with about ¼ pound of cooked chorizo.

Dairy-Free / Gluten-Free / Nut-Free

Camarones Guisados Criollos

Creole Shrimp Stew

MAKES: 8 servings | **PREP TIME:** 5 minutes | **COOK TIME:** 25 minutes

3 tablespoons achiote oil (see page 117)

¼ cup sofrito (see page 116)

3 bay leaves

½ cup alcaparrado (see page 124)

3 ounces cubed ham

1 (16-ounce) can whole peeled tomatoes, drained and chopped

1 cup tomato sauce

2 pounds medium shrimp, peeled and deveined

Salt

Pepper

Puerto Ricans like their seasonings and flavors; we use a lot of them in most of our meals. Another cuisine with some great flavors is Creole. It's only natural that Puerto Ricans would borrow some of their great seasonings and flavors and put our own twist on them. This shrimp stew is a beautiful blending of two styles of cooking that come together easily and deliciously.

1. Heat achiote oil in a large pot over medium heat. Add the sofrito, bay leaves, alcaparrado, and ham, and sauté for 2 to 3 minutes. Set aside.

2. Drain the whole tomatoes and roughly chop them. Add the tomato sauce and chopped tomatoes to the same pot and return to heat, bringing to a boil.

3. Reduce the heat to medium and add the shrimp, cooking for about 5 minutes until they become pink and opaque. Add salt and pepper to taste, cook for a couple of minutes to meld the flavors, then serve.

Bacalao Guisado

Codfish Stew

MAKES: 8 servings | **PREP TIME:** 15 minutes | **COOK TIME:** 1 hour

Salted water

½ pound peeled yuca

1½ pounds cod fillet

1 tablespoon olive oil

2 tablespoons sofrito (see page 116)

1 cup diced onion

1 green pepper, diced

½ cup tomato sauce

1 tablespoon sazón (see page 121)

½ cup pimento stuffed green olives

My dad always scolded me whenever I said the name of this dish. I used the full name, *Bacalao Guisado*, and he would always tell me that no one on the island says the full name! It was shortened and popularized as *Bacalao Guisao*, and he liked to throw jabs at me whenever I made it, asking how he was able to teach me how to make it right but couldn't teach me how to say it right.

1. Fill a large pot with salted water (use no more than ½ teaspoon salt) and bring to a boil. Place peeled yuca and deboned cod fillets into the water and boil for 35 to 40 minutes.

2. Drain the water, then break the codfish into bite-size chunks and chop the yuca into about 1-inch cubes.

3. Heat olive oil in a large pot over medium heat. Once the oil starts to sizzle, add in the sofrito and sauté for about 1 minute until it becomes fragrant. Then add onions and green pepper, and cook for about 5 minutes until they become tender. Add tomato sauce, sazón, olives, cod, and yuca. Reduce heat to low, cook for 15 minutes, then serve.

SERVING TIP: The Guanimes (see page 77) are a perfect side for this dish, or you can serve it over white rice with some tostones (see page 38) for dipping.

VARIATION TIP: Classic salted codfish is used for this recipe. I tend to make it with fresh cod, but if you are going with salted, make sure to soak in water for a day to remove the salt. You will want to change the water out a couple of times during that period. You can also easily use potatoes in place of yuca if you like.

Pasteles

MAKES: 18 servings | **PREP TIME:** 35 minutes plus 1 hour chill time | **COOK TIME:** 2 hours 20 minutes

FOR THE MASA

10 green bananas

2 green plantains

2 pounds yautía root

½ pound potatoes

2 tablespoons milk

¼ cup achiote oil (see page 117)

Salt

FOR THE FILLING

3 pounds pork shoulder

3½ tablespoons sofrito (see page 116)

1 (8-ounce) can tomato sauce

2 cups water

1 tablespoon sazón (see page 121)

Salt

Pepper

18 banana leaves (see page 131 for preparation)

Achiote oil (see page 117)

Pasteles are the go-to dish for Puerto Ricans during the Christmas season. While pasteles are made in several Caribbean countries, the Puerto Rican version is pretty unique. It blends several cuisines, including the *masa* (dough) based on what the native Taínos made from cassava root. This cultural combination of foods over the centuries has created a singular and tasty holiday dish that everyone loves.

TO MAKE THE MASA

Peel and cube the bananas, plantains, yautía, and potatoes. Put into a food processor and add milk, oil, and salt to taste. Blend until smooth. Keep covered and refrigerate for at least an hour.

TO MAKE THE FILLING

Cut the pork shoulder into very small cubes. Put into a large pot and add sofrito, tomato sauce, water, sazón, and salt and pepper to taste. Bring to a boil, then reduce the heat and simmer for about 45 minutes. Let cool enough to be handled by hand.

TO ASSEMBLE THE PASTELES

1. Place a prepared banana leaf on a piece of parchment paper and brush with a light coating of achiote oil. Spoon about ¾ cup of the masa into the center of the leaf and spread it out to form a thin circle with no breaks in it. Then scoop about ½ cup of the pork filling on top of the masa.

2. Holding the parchment paper edge farthest from you carefully fold it in half toward you. The open end of the banana leaf should be facing you; fold that in about 1½ inches. Next fold in the side to your right toward the center, and then fold the left side over that. What you should have will essentially look like a banana leaf envelope with no sides open. Wrap a piece of cooking twine around the pastel and tie it shut with a bow.

3. Bring a large pot (it can be the same pot you used to make the pork shoulder) of salted water (use no more than ½ teaspoon of salt) to a boil and carefully place the wrapped pasteles into the water. Make sure the pasteles are completely immersed. Allow to boil for about 1½ hours.

4. Remove from water, let cool, and serve.

MAKE-AHEAD TIP: While not complicated, making pasteles is a long process. If you would like to break it up, complete steps 1 through 4 and then freeze until you are ready to cook them. Let them thaw before boiling, or boil for an extra roughly 30 minutes. If they aren't done yet don't worry; simply rewrap them and boil them a little longer.

Rum Cake,
Page 100

6

Sheet Pan, Casserole Dish, and Bakery

WHILE THE STOVE TOP IS GREAT FOR MINGLING FLAVORS together in a skillet or getting a pot of stew going, sometimes you need to be able to just throw something in the oven and walk away so you can get other things done. Puerto Rican families tend to be large, and big families need a lot of attention, after all. Puerto Rican cuisine has plenty of these types of recipes. In this chapter we will take a look at the simplicity of sheet pan and casserole dish recipes from our little island, and explore easy versions of some of our most iconic baked goods.

Mofongo Stuffing

MAKES: 8 servings | **PREP TIME:** 15 minutes | **COOK TIME:** 35 minutes

1 tablespoon plus
1 cup olive oil

1 onion, chopped

4 garlic cloves, chopped

½ cup chopped ají
dulce peppers

1 ají caballero
pepper, chopped

2 medium toma-
toes, chopped

2 tablespoons butter

1 cup water

4 green plantains

1 ounce chicharrónes
(see page 118)

While not an old-school traditional Puerto Rican recipe, Mofongo Stuffing has crept up in popularity in the last decade. Showing the versatility of our cuisine, it is a fusion between classic Puerto Rican Mofongo and American Thanksgiving–style stuffing to create a new side that works with about any meal—no need to relegate it to holidays.

1. Preheat your oven to 375°F. Heat 1 tablespoon oil in a sauté pan or skillet over medium heat and add onion, garlic, and peppers, and sauté for 5 minutes until the vegetables begin to soften. Add in tomatoes, butter, and 1 cup of water. Bring mixture to a boil, then reduce heat and simmer for 10 minutes, stirring occasionally.

2. Let mixture cool slightly, then transfer to a food processor and blend until smooth.

3. Cut both ends off of plantains. Find one of the ribs that runs lengthwise and slice along it. Peel the skin off using your fingers or a spoon. Slice the plantains into 1-inch sections.

4. Heat about 1 cup olive oil over medium to high heat. Place plantain slices into heated oil (use enough oil to cover the plantains) and fry for 2 to 3 minutes per side. Remove from pan and place on a paper towel to drain excess oil and cool.

5. In a large bowl combine vegetable mixture, fried plantains, and chicharrónes, mashing it like you would potatoes. Transfer to a baking dish and bake for about 15 minutes. Remove from oven, let cool, and serve.

SUBSTITUTION TIP: If you can't find some of the peppers listed above you can use sweet Italian peppers in place of ají dulce peppers, and while habanero peppers have more heat, you can use a small one or a fresno pepper in place of the ají caballero pepper. See page 118 for a chicharrónes recipe, but in a pinch, you can use pork rinds.

Pan de Mallorca

Sweet Bread Rolls

MAKES: 10 rolls | **PREP TIME:** 3 hours | **COOK TIME:** 30 minutes

---

½ cup warm milk

1½ cups warm water

1 (¼ ounce) package dry yeast

8 egg yolks

¾ cup granulated sugar

1 cup (2 sticks) melted butter

6½ cups bread flour

1 teaspoon salt

Powdered sugar

Another recipe that borrows its origins from another culture is *Pan de Mallorca*. Known in English as Mallorca bread, this was originally a Spanish recipe that started out as *ensaimada*, a bread fried in pork lard. Once here it was embraced and changed into the sweet bakery treat it is today. If you are lucky enough to travel to Puerto Rico, visiting an island bakery for Pan de Mallorca is a must. These rolls are perfect for breakfast and go great with your morning coffee.

1. Pour milk, water, and dry yeast into a large bowl and let rest for 1 to 2 minutes. The mixture will form a foamy head as the yeast activates.

2. While this liquid mixture is resting, in another large bowl whisk together the eggs, sugar, and butter until completely combined. Pour the yeast mixture into your egg mixture and whisk until combined.

3. Add in your flour and salt, and knead the dough. If you have a stand mixer with a dough hook, you can use this instead of kneading by hand. You want to knead it until it is tacky. Transfer to a bowl, cover with a kitchen cloth, and rest on the counter for about 2 hours. By the time it's ready it should have doubled in size.

4. Lightly flour your working area and place the dough on it. Sprinkle dough with a little flour as well. Break the dough into 10 equal pieces and roll them out into long cords, about ½ inch thick. Coil the cords into circular buns, tucking the end of the cord under the bottom. Place rolls onto a parchment-lined baking sheet, cover, and rest for 45 minutes.

continued on next page

5. Preheat your oven to 350°F. Lightly brush each roll with a little melted butter and bake for 20 to 25 minutes. Remove from the oven and let buns cool to room temperature, then sprinkle with powdered sugar and serve.

COOKING TIPS: You want your water and milk temperatures to be between 120° to 130°F. This is important; if they're too cool the yeast won't rise, if they're too hot you'll kill the yeast. I have done the latter many times while learning to cook with yeast. If kneading by hand, it's important not to overwork the dough as kneading it too much can overheat the yeast. Instead of letting the dough rest on the counter, you can refrigerate it overnight while it rises.

SUBSTITUTION TIP: If you don't have access to bread flour, you can use all-purpose flour.

Albondigon

Meatloaf

MAKES: 6 servings | **PREP TIME:** 10 minutes | **COOK TIME:** 1 hour

1½ cups bread crumbs

½ teaspoon cumin

½ teaspoon coriander

1 teaspoon sazón
 (see page 121)

1 tablespoon adobo
 (see page 120)

2 eggs

2 tablespoons sofrito
 (see page 116)

2 tablespoons ketchup

2 tablespoons
 chopped cilantro

¼ chopped onion

2 pounds ground beef

Sometimes there is nothing like a dinner of simple comfort food, and nothing says comfort food like a great meatloaf. Like most well-known dishes, Puerto Ricans put their own twist on meatloaf. Adding in some of the flavors and seasonings unique to the island really puts this classic dish over the top.

1. Preheat your oven to 350°F. In a large bowl whisk together breadcrumbs, cumin, coriander, sazón, and adobo.

2. Add in eggs, sofrito, and ketchup, and combine. Then add cilantro and onions, mixing until completely incorporated. Lastly, add in the ground beef. (This is added last so the beef doesn't get overworked and the meatloaf stays tender.)

3. Once the mixture is completely incorporated, place it on a baking sheet and form into a loaf shape. Pour about ½ cup of water onto your sheet pan and bake for 45 minutes to 1 hour. Remove from the oven and serve while hot.

Pastelón

Plantain Lasagna

MAKES: 6 servings | **PREP TIME:** 15 minutes | **COOK TIME:** 40 minutes

5 ripe yellow plantains

Oil

4 beaten eggs

2 cups picadillo
(see page 123)

1½ cups shredded
mozzarella

1½ cups shredded
Swiss cheese

My brother is a huge fan of lasagna, so when my dad told us Puerto Rico has a layered casserole comparable to the beloved Italian dish, he couldn't wait to try it. I just had to dig in and learn how to make this to one-up my little brother. The bonus is that it's really easy to make and has an unbelievably great flavor.

1. Preheat your oven to 350°F. Cut both ends off of the plantains. Find one of the ribs that runs lengthwise and slice along it. Peel the skin off using your fingers or a spoon, then slice lengthwise, ending up with 4 strips per plantain.

2. Heat the oil in a large sauté pan or skillet over medium heat. Carefully lay the plantain strips in the oil and fry for 3 to 4 minutes per side. Place on paper towels to drain excess oil.

3. Line the bottom of a 9-by-13-inch baking dish with half the fried plantains. Pour half of the egg wash over the plantains making sure to coat them evenly. Spoon the picadillo over the egg, then evenly spread half of each cheese over the picadillo. Layer the rest of the plantains and egg wash, and top with the remainder of the cheeses. Bake for 20 to 25 minutes until the cheese is completely melted.

SUBSTITUTION TIP: Mozzarella and Swiss are my favorites, but you can use any cheese you like on this one.

Quesitos

Cream Cheese Turnovers

MAKES: 9 pastries | **PREP TIME:** 10 minutes | **COOK TIME:** 15 minutes

1 sheet thawed puff pastry

1 (8-ounce) package
  cream cheese

¼ cup granulated sugar

1 teaspoon vanilla

1 beaten egg white

1 tablespoon honey

Quesitos may be one of the most popular baked treats on the island. So much so that the stores and bakeries that sell them have started calling them by the name of their packaging: *Bomboneras*, which literally means "candy box" or "chocolate box." These are the perfect little dessert or sweet treat any time of the day.

1. Preheat your oven to 350°F. On a lightly floured surface, lay out the thawed puff pastry sheet. Using a pizza cutter or knife, cut into 9 equal pieces.

2. In a small bowl whip together cream cheese, sugar, and vanilla. Scoop about 1 tablespoon of the cheese mixture into the center of each pastry. Fold each corner inward so they overlap over the cheese.

3. Place pastries on a parchment-lined baking sheet, brush with beaten egg white, and sprinkle each with a pinch of sugar. Bake for 15 to 20 minutes until they puff up and become golden in color. Let cool and brush with honey before serving.

VARIATION TIP: You can add a little guava paste to the cheese before closing up the pastries to add a fruity flavor.

Nut-Free / Vegetarian

Budín de Pan

Puerto Rican Bread Pudding

MAKES: 8 servings | **PREP TIME:** 10 minutes | **COOK TIME:** 25 minutes

16 slices of bread

1 (14-ounce) can condensed milk

1 cup evaporated milk

5 eggs, beaten

¼ cup melted butter

Puerto Rican bread pudding is one of those recipes that has as many ways to cook it as there are Puerto Ricans themselves. Each version has a little twist to it that makes it unique. Over the years I've played with different ways to make it, and I've come up with this one that I think has the best combination of flavors.

1. Preheat your oven to 350°F. Tear the bread slices into large chunks in a large bowl then pour condensed milk and evaporated milk over the bread. Mix together, soaking the bread pieces. Then mix in the beaten eggs and melted butter and combine well.

2. Put everything into a greased Bundt pan, and bake for about 25 minutes. Pierce with a toothpick to make sure it's done (if it is, the toothpick will come out clean). Let cool before removing from the pan and serving.

VARIATION TIP: Feel free to add raisins or other dried fruit to your taste. If using, mix them in with the eggs.

Nut-Free / Vegetarian

Puerto Rican Shortbread Cookies

MAKES: 20 cookies | **PREP TIME:** 10 minutes | **COOK TIME:** 25 minutes

½ cup (1 stick) butter

½ cup shortening

½ cup granulated sugar

1 beaten egg yolk

1 teaspoon vanilla

Salt

2¼ cups flour

1 (10-ounce) can guava paste

When my aunt and uncle visited from Puerto Rico for the first time, my brother and I were little kids. Aunt Juanita would be at our house all day cooking, not only making meals for our whole family, but also making little treats for my brother and I. *Mantecaditos* were one of the treats she made for us often, and they always bring back great childhood memories whenever I make them myself.

1. Preheat your oven to 350°F. In a large bowl cream together the butter, shortening, and sugar, and egg yolk until it starts to form peaks. Mix in vanilla, salt, and flour until completely combined.

2. Scoop about 1 tablespoon of dough at a time onto a parchment-lined baking sheet. Press your thumb into the center of the cookie to create an indent, and place about ½-inch cube of guava paste into each indent. Bake for 20 to 25 minutes. Remove from oven and place cookies on a wire rack to cool before serving.

VARIATION TIP: Instead of guava paste, you can use just about any jelly you like.

Tres Leches Cake

Three Milks Cake

MAKES: 12 servings | **PREP TIME:** 25 minutes | **COOK TIME:** 45 minutes plus 1 hour chill time

5 eggs, yolks and whites separated

1 cup granulated sugar

1 teaspoon vanilla

1¼ cups flour

¾ teaspoon salt

1 teaspoon baking powder

1 (12-ounce) can evaporated milk

1 (14-ounce) can sweetened condensed milk

¼ cup whole milk

1½ cup whipped cream

1 tablespoon powdered sugar

This is a popular Latin cake that my brother and I didn't try until we were young adults. Both of us agree that we missed out on a lot of great cake during our childhood! More and more people are trying different variations of the *Tres Leches* but truly there is nothing like the original.

1. Preheat your oven to 350°F. In a small bowl, beat egg yolks until they become light and fluffy. Add sugar and vanilla and mix until combined.

2. In a separate bowl, beat the egg whites until they form peaks (you may want to use an electric mixer for this). Fold whites into the yolks with a spatula, then slowly fold the flour, salt, and baking powder into the mixture.

3. Pour batter into a greased and floured 9-by-13-inch baking dish, and bake for 35 to 40 minutes. Test cake with a toothpick to make sure it is done. Remove cake from oven and allow to cool completely.

4. In a medium bowl whisk together the three milks. Using a small wooden skewer, poke holes in the cake and pour the milk mixture over the whole cake. Place the cake in the refrigerator for at least 1 hour to chill.

5. Once chilled, in a small bowl beat together the whipped cream and powdered sugar. Spread the mixture over the cake before serving.

VARIATION TIP: For a real island taste, replace the sweetened condensed milk with coconut cream, usually found in the canned goods aisle of most grocery stores.

Cazuela

Sweet Potato Pudding

MAKES: 10 servings | **PREP TIME:** 15 minutes | **COOK TIME:** 1 hour 25 minutes

1½ pounds sweet potatoes

1½ pounds pumpkin

Water

1½ teaspoons salt

1 cup coconut milk

1½ cup granulated sugar

½ teaspoon ground cloves

½ teaspoon cinnamon

½ teaspoon ginger

¼ cup rice flour

3 beaten eggs

I ended the last chapter with a Puerto Rican holiday must-have, Pasteles. This recipe is another holiday classic, this time a dessert, *Cazuela*. Just about everywhere else, Cazuela is a stew or a one-pot meal. Of course, though, in Puerto Rico we have to be different. Our version is a crustless sweet potato and squash pie that's perfect for the Christmas season.

1. Preheat your oven to 350°F. Peel the pumpkin and sweet potatoes and cut into 2-inch cubes. Bring a large pot of water to boil, enough to cover the pumpkin and sweet potatoes, and boil for about 20 minutes.

2. Drain the water. Put pumpkin and sweet potatoes in a large bowl with the salt, coconut milk, sugar, ground cloves, cinnamon, ginger, flour, and eggs, and beat with a mixer until smooth and incorporated.

3. Pour the batter into a greased 8-by-8-inch baking dish. Bake for 1 hour.

4. Remove from the oven, turn the broiler on, and place under the broiler for about 2 minutes so it gets a nice crust on it. Once done baking, place in the refrigerator to cool before serving.

VARIATION TIP: Classically this recipe is made with calabasa (a Caribbean squash) rather than pumpkin. Calabasas can be hard to find sometimes so I use pumpkin, but if you can find them use those instead.

Bizcochos de Ron

Rum Cake

MAKES: 8 servings | **PREP TIME:** 10 minutes | **COOK TIME:** 1 hour

FOR THE CAKE

½ cup chopped pecans

1 (18½-ounce) box
  yellow cake mix

1 (3¼-ounce) box instant
  vanilla pudding

½ cup dark rum

½ cup vegetable oil

4 eggs

FOR THE RUM GLAZE

1 cup granulated sugar

½ cup (1 stick) butter

¼ cup dark rum

¼ cup water

Rum cake is a popular dessert no matter where you go. In Puerto Rico it's usually enjoyed as a holiday treat. The Puerto Rican version, *Bizcochos de Ron*, not only has rum in the batter but it's also typically soaked in rum glaze as well.

TO MAKE THE CAKE

1. Preheat your oven to 350°F. Grease a Bundt pan, then sprinkle the chopped pecans across the bottom of the pan.

2. In a large bowl beat together the cake mix, vanilla pudding, rum, oil, and eggs until completely combined. Pour cake batter into prepared Bundt pan over the pecans, place in the oven, and bake for one hour.

TO MAKE THE GLAZE

1. About 10 minutes before the cake is finished baking, mix together the sugar, butter, rum, and water in a small saucepan. Bring to a boil, then turn down the heat and simmer for 3 to 4 minutes, stirring constantly.

2. Test cake with a toothpick to make sure it's done, then remove from the oven. Invert the pan and slide the cake out onto a serving plate. Pour the hot glaze over the cake and allow it to soak in and cool before serving.

VARIATION TIP: If you like raisins you can add them into this recipe. Soak the raisins in rum for at least a day before mixing them into the batter.

Sancocho,
Page 110

7

Slow Cooker/ Pressure Cooker Recipes

ONE OF THE CENTRAL THEMES IN PUERTO RICAN COOKING IS feeding a lot of people with a single dish. I covered some of these types of recipes in the one-pot section of the book. Here, we'll take a deeper dive into some recipes that you may find in a traditional Puerto Rican home. These recipes are the same traditional ones my dad taught me, but I simplified them by creating simple set-it-and-forget-it slow-cooker and quick pressure cooker versions of them. There's no need to slave over a hot stove all day to achieve that old-style feel of island cooking. Now you can spend time with your family while cooking for them, instead of spending all your time and attention focusing solely on the process. You get more time to enjoy what is great about Puerto Rican food: the togetherness of family.

Dairy-Free / Gluten-Free / Nut-Free / Vegan

Guineos en Escabeche

Pickled Plantains

MAKES: 4 servings | **PREP TIME:** 4 hours | **COOK TIME:** 4 hours

1 red onion, sliced

6 garlic cloves, minced

2 cups olive oil

1 cup apple cider vinegar

½ cup alcaparrado
(see page 124)

½ teaspoon peppercorns

10 green bananas

1 avocado, diced

Out of all the Puerto Rican dishes I learned to prepare and serve, the one that I never truly understood was *Guineos en Escabeche.* While I love the flavor of bananas, using them in this recipe over plantains seemed a bit odd. As I got older and started thinking more about healthier cooking, I came to realize what a perfect vegan, low-calorie recipe Guineos en Escabeche truly is as it's quick, easy, and can be eaten as a salad or snack.

1. Put sliced onion, garlic, olive oil, apple cider vinegar, alcaparrado, and peppercorns into the slow cooker and stir. Set cooker to high and cook for 3 hours. (This is a good "set and forget" recipe, giving you time to do other things while the ingredients are pickling.)

2. Cut the ends off of the bananas. Sliding a knife lengthwise down one of the spines to create an opening, use either your thumb or a spoon to remove the peel from the unripe banana. Slice each banana into 1-inch sections. Place them into the slow cooker and cook on low for another hour. Bananas should be tender but still firm.

3. Allow to cool enough to handle and pour into a large container. Add avocados and carefully mix together. Refrigerate for at least 4 hours before serving.

Frijoles Negros y Arroz Blanco

Black Beans and White Rice

MAKES: 4 to 6 servings | **PREP TIME:** 10 minutes | **COOK TIME:** 8 hours

2 cups dried black beans

¾ cup sofrito
  (see page 116)

½ cup chopped
  canned tomato

¾ teaspoon cumin

½ teaspoon oregano

½ Spanish onion, diced

2 garlic cloves, minced

4 cups water

Salt

Pepper

½ cup chopped cilantro

Though there are several staples in Latin American cuisine, rice and beans reigns supreme. As you've learned throughout this book, most Puerto Rican dinners are usually served with some type of rice and beans, whether it's Arroz con Gandules or Arroz Blanco con Habichuelas (white rice with beans). This recipe, however, is one that my brother has always preferred over either of those, and is probably the reason why many in the family think he might secretly be from the Dominican Republic, where black beans are more popular. As with kidney and pinto beans, black beans are packed with nutrients and high in fiber—truly a superfood. If you enjoy this recipe as my brother does, make it for breakfast with a couple of eggs on the side.

1. Rinse and remove any debris from black beans. Add sofrito, tomatoes, cumin, oregano, onions, and garlic to your slow cooker along with 4 cups of water. Stir.

2. Set the cooker to low and cook for 8 hours. The beans should be soft but still firm enough to hold their shape. Turn the heat off, add salt and pepper to taste, and stir in the cilantro. Serve over freshly cooked white rice.

Carne Guisada

Beef Stew

MAKES: 8 servings | **PREP TIME:** 15 minutes | **COOK TIME:** 25 minutes

3 pounds cubed beef

2 tablespoons adobo (see page 120)

1 teaspoon cumin

1 tablespoon flour

4 garlic cloves, diced

4 tablespoons sofrito (see page 116)

1 cup chopped cilantro

1 (8-ounce) can tomato sauce

1½ teaspoon sazón (see page 121)

¼ cup alcaparrado (see page 124)

3 peeled potatoes, cut into 1-inch cubes

Just about every culture has its own version of a classic beef stew. This Puerto Rican version was the first stew my dad taught me to make, so it will always hold a special place in my heart on top of quickly becoming one of my favorite fall dishes. While it is a complete meal by itself, I love serving it over some white rice. This recipe perfectly lends itself to cooking in a pressure cooker.

1. Place cubed beef in a large bowl and sprinkle with adobo, cumin, and flour, and toss to coat. Select sauté on the pressure cooker, and add in the seasoned beef in batches, browning on all sides, about 5 minutes per batch.

2. Add garlic, sofrito, cilantro, tomato sauce, sazón, and alcaparrado to the pressure cooker. Stir everything together and lock the lid into place. Cook on high pressure for 10 minutes. Let the pressure release naturally for about 5 minutes, then do a quick release.

3. Add in the cubed potatoes and replace the lid. Set to high pressure and cook for 2 more minutes. Allow the pressure to release naturally.

VARIATION TIP: You can also make this the traditional stove top way. Sear the meat over medium to high heat in a large pot or caldero, then remove the meat and add in sofrito, cilantro, and garlic, and cook for 2 to 3 minutes. Add in seasonings and enough water to cover meat, then cover and simmer for 30 minutes. Add in potatoes and cook, covered, for another 20 minutes.

Sopa de Habichuelas Blancas

White Bean Soup

MAKES: 6 servings | **PREP TIME:** 10 minutes | **COOK TIME:** 50 minutes

½ pound chopped bacon

½ pound dry white
navy beans

1 garlic clove, minced

¼ cup sofrito
(see page 116)

½ cup alcaparrado
(see page 124)

1 cup tomato sauce

8 cups chicken broth

2 potatoes, peeled
and cubed

What do Puerto Ricans eat when the flu bug strikes or when the temperature dips? Out of the various soups we enjoy together, *sopa de habichuelas blancas* always hits the spot for me. Think of your grandmother's special soup that helps chase away a chill and replenish your vitality without leaving you overly full. The starchiness of the white beans gives this soup its distinct texture and will have you scraping the bowl to get every last morsel. You can also experiment with different herbs and spices you like and make this recipe your own, the way I did by turning it into a pressure cooker soup.

1. Cook bacon until desired doneness, then remove from pan and set aside.

2. Rinse beans thoroughly, then place beans, garlic, sofrito, alcaparrado, tomato sauce, and chicken broth into the pressure cooker. Set the cooker to high pressure for 35 minutes, with a complete natural release.

3. After 35 minutes stir in the potatoes, replace the lid, and set to high pressure; cook for another 3 minutes, then do a five-minute natural release followed by a quick release.

VARIATION TIP: If cooking on the stove top, sauté bacon in a large pot until crispy. Remove from the pot and add in sofrito, garlic, and alcaparrado. Cook 2 to 3 minutes until the garlic becomes fragrant. Add in the remainder of the ingredients and stir. Bring to a simmer, cover, and cook for about 20 minutes, then serve.

Dairy-Free / Nut-free

Asopao de Pollo

Chicken Soup

MAKES: 6 servings | **PREP TIME:** 15 minutes | **COOK TIME:** 10 minutes

---

8 to 10 cups salted water

1½ cups angel hair pasta

2 tablespoons olive oil

2 chicken breasts

3 chicken thighs

4 garlic cloves, minced

2 potatoes, cubed

3 carrots, chopped

1 bunch of
   cilantro, chopped

½ cup sofrito
   (see page 116)

½ cup alcaparrado
   (see page 124)

2 tablespoons
   chicken bouillon

1½ teaspoon sazón
   (see page 121)

When I learned this recipe, my wife took it over and made it her own. I made this for her once and it became a staple in our kitchen. Puerto Rican chicken soup is now her be-all and end-all of soup. The rich flavors that the sazón and sofrito bring to something as simple as chicken soup is nothing short of amazing. The recipe is also so easy to tweak to make it completely to your taste.

1. Bring about 3 cups of salted water (use no more than ½ teaspoon salt) to a boil. Add in noodles and cook for about 12 minutes. Drain and set aside.

2. Drizzle 2 tablespoons of olive oil into the pressure cooker and set to sauté. While oil is heating, cut chicken into about 1-inch bite-size cubes. Brown the chicken in the oil; don't cook it all the way through, just enough to give it a nice sear.

3. Add the garlic, potatoes, carrots, cilantro, sofrito, alcaparrado, chicken bouillon, and sazón into the pressure cooker with the chicken. Lock lid into place, set to high pressure, and cook for 4 minutes. When finished, let the pressure release naturally for 5 minutes, then finish with a quick release. When the valve drops remove the lid and stir in the pre-cooked noodles, then serve.

COOKING TIP: I like to cook the noodles separately because I think they become too soft when preparing them in the pressure cooker. You can add in the noodles with the rest of the ingredients if you like them softer.

VARIATION TIP: You can add rice to the recipe to create a heartier meal. With about 2 hours left on the cook time, pour in 1½ cups rice, re-cover, and allow to finish cooking for another 2 hours.

Pollo Guisado

Chicken Stew

MAKES: 6 servings | **PREP TIME:** 15 minutes | **COOK TIME:** 4 to 8 hours

3 chicken breasts, cubed

2 potatoes, cubed

½ cup alcaparrado
(see page 124)

3 carrots, chopped

1½ teaspoons sazón
(see page 121)

1 teaspoon adobo
(see page 120)

½ teaspoon cumin

½ teaspoon oregano

1 (8-ounce) can
tomato sauce

Water

More so than any other main course, I believe that *Pollo Guisado* encapsulates what it means to enjoy Puerto Rican cuisine. Whether for breakfast, lunch, dinner, or a midnight raid of the leftovers in the refrigerator, this Borinquen chicken stew will provide you with the *sabor* of Puerto Rico in every bite. As mentioned in the introduction to this book, Puerto Rican culture is defined by the diversity of cultures within it, and the flavors present in Pollo Guisado are a representation of many of them. Served with rice or on its own, this is an all-time favorite.

Put the chicken, potatoes, alcaparrado, carrots, sazón, adobe, cumin, oregano, and tomato sauce into the slow cooker with enough water to submerge everything, and stir. Set to low and cook for 8 hours, set to high for 4 hours. Serve with rice or by itself.

Sancocho

Puerto Rican Stew

MAKES: 10 servings | **PREP TIME:** 20 minutes | **COOK TIME:** 8 hours

1½ pounds top round beef

1 yuca, peeled
and chopped

3 potatoes, peeled
and chopped

1 yellow plantain, sliced

2 green plantains, sliced

2 ears corn

5 garlic cloves, minced

⅓ cup chopped
Spanish onions

⅓ cup chopped
green pepper

½ cup chopped cilantro

1 tablespoon adobo
(see page 120)

½ cup sofrito
(see page 116)

4 quarts (16 cups)
beef broth

Salt

Pepper

There's a great beef stew earlier in this chapter, but don't think that *sancocho* is just another beef stew; this is one of the most traditional stews of the island. When you talk about down-home comfort foods, nothing in all of Puerto Rican cuisine comes close to sancocho. Whenever my Puerto Rican friends find out I'm making it, I get calls from them asking when they can come get some. If you're looking for a real comfort food, this is the recipe for you.

1. Chop beef, yuca, and potatoes into roughly 1-inch cubes. Slice the plantains into about 1-inch pieces and the ears of corn into 2-inch pieces.

2. Add the beef, yuca, potatoes, plantains, corn, garlic, onions, peppers, cilantro, adobo, sofrito, and beef broth to the slow cooker and stir to combine, adding salt and pepper to taste. Set on low and cook for 6 to 8 hours, until all the starches are tender, then serve.

VARIATION TIP: To make this on the stove top, heat a couple of tablespoons of oil in a caldero or Dutch oven. Sauté the garlic and onions until the garlic becomes fragrant. Add cubed beef and brown on all sides. Then add green peppers, cilantro, sofrito, seasonings, and 4 cups of the beef broth. Bring to a boil, then reduce heat and simmer for 20 minutes. Add the rest of the ingredients and beef broth and cook until all the starches are tender.

Albondigas

Meatballs

MAKES: 5 servings | **PREP TIME:** 10 minutes | **COOK TIME:** 6 to 8 hours

FOR THE MEATBALLS

1 pound ground beef

½ cup bread crumbs

½ cup sofrito
  (see page 116)

1 beaten egg

½ bunch cilantro, chopped

1 tablespoon oil

FOR THE SAUCE

4 cups beef broth

1 tablespoon sofrito
  (see page 116)

1 (8-ounce) can
  tomato sauce

¼ cup alcaparrado
  (see page 124)

These cool little meatballs are simple to make but versatile. Serve them over some rice and you have a great dinner, or throw them on a toasted roll and you have the perfect meatball sandwich for lunch. My little brother usually just toasts a little Italian bread to eat with them. He loves using the bread to sop up the sauce, not letting any of it go to waste.

TO MAKE THE MEATBALLS

1. Combine the ground beef, bread crumbs, sofrito, egg, and cilantro in a medium bowl. Form the mixture into roughly 1½-inch balls.

2. On the stove top heat 1 tablespoon oil in a sauté pan or skillet over medium to high heat. Sear the meatballs on all sides, 2 to 3 minutes per side. Remove the meatballs and set them aside.

TO MAKE THE SAUCE

Add the beef broth, sofrito, tomato sauce, and alcaparrado into the slow cooker and mix. Add meatballs to the sauce, set to low heat, and cook for 6 to 8 hours.

> **VARIATION TIP:** To make these on the stove top combine all the sauce ingredients in a caldero or Dutch oven, then make the meatball mixture. Place the formed meatballs into the sauce and bring to a simmer. Cover and cook for 25 to 30 minutes.

Bistec Encebollado

Steak and Onions

MAKES: 6 servings | **PREP TIME:** 5 minutes | **COOK TIME:** 8 hours

2 pounds flank steak

Salt

Pepper

2 Spanish onions, sliced

2 garlic cloves, minced

¼ cup red wine vinegar

1 cup beef broth

2 teaspoons oregano

1 tablespoon cumin

Bistec Encebollado is a very typical lunch or dinner recipe in most Latin American countries. Spanish onions tend to have a sweeter flavor than many other onions and balance out the vinegar, garlic, and oregano. On the stove top I would never cook a steak to well-done; but here, the moisture gets locked in while in the slow cooker, ensuring an extremely tender cut of meat.

1. Slice steak into long thin strips and place into the slow cooker. Season with salt and pepper to taste. Cover the steak with the sliced onion and minced garlic.

2. In a small bowl mix together the vinegar, beef broth, oregano, and cumin and pour over steak and onions. Set slow cooker to low and cook for 8 hours.

VARIATION TIP: To make this on the stove top, mix together red wine vinegar, ½ cup beef broth, oregano, cumin, and garlic. Place the steak in the marinade, making sure it is completely coated. Cover and place in the refrigerator for at least 8 hours. After marinating, heat 2 tablespoons of oil in a skillet and sauté onions for 3 to 4 minutes. Pour in the other ½ cup of beef broth and let the onions cook, absorbing the broth for another 7 to 10 minutes. Remove the onions from the pan, and in the same pan cook the steak to your preferred temperature.

Dairy-Free / Gluten-Free / Nut-Free

Pernil

Pork Shoulder

MAKES: 8 to 10 servings | **PREP TIME:** 4 to 8 hours | **COOK TIME:** 8 hours

---

6 pounds pork shoulder

2 heads garlic

½ cup olive oil

¼ cup white vinegar

2 teaspoons sazón
  (see page 121)

1 teaspoon adobo
  (see page 120)

1 teaspoon oregano

Pepper

This is the recipe I know a lot of people have been waiting for (well, anyone who knows Puerto Rican cooking definitely has been waiting for this one!). Everyone has certain go-to meals or dishes that make them think of their family and togetherness. Well, the three recipes guaranteed to bring Puerto Rican families together are arroz con gandules, pasteles, and pernil.

1. Make slits in all sides of the pork shoulder. Peel 1 head of garlic and stuff the cloves into the slits you just made.

2. Put the olive oil, vinegar, sazón, adobo, oregano, and pepper in a food processor and blend until smooth. Coat the pork shoulder with this mixture, then wrap in plastic wrap and rest in the refrigerator at least overnight.

3. Remove the pork from its wrapping and place in the slow cooker on low for 8 hours. Slice, then serve.

VARIATION TIP: Traditionally (the way my dad taught me), pernil is roasted in the oven to give it a crispy skin. To cook it this way, once the pork is done marinating, preheat your oven to 325°F. Once the oven has reached temperature place the pork shoulder in a deep baking dish with at least 2-inch-high sides. Roast for 3½ hours, then turn the heat up to 450°F. Pour about ¼ to ½ cup water into the pan and cook another 35 minutes or until the skin is as crispy as you like it.

INGREDIENT TIP: Choose a nice marbled pork shoulder with plenty of fat as this will help keep it moist during cooking.

Chimichurri,
Page 130

8

Staples

WE USE A LOT OF TRIED AND TRUE INGREDIENTS IN PUERTO Rican cuisine, so we always have a few items on hand. Some of them we use so frequently that we tend to prepare them in larger quantities and keep them for when we're ready to use them. Throughout this book you'll see a lot of ingredients over and over again, such as adobo and sofrito, and each time you see one of these staples in a recipe, the page number where you can find the recipe will be listed next to it. You can find these staples in the store or online, but why buy them when they're so simple to make and end up tasting so much better when you create them from scratch? Having these staples on hand will make everything easier—and make you a pro at cooking Puerto Rican cuisine.

Puerto Rican Sofrito

MAKES: 4 cups | **PREP TIME:** 15 minutes

1 bunch cilantro

1 red bell pepper

2 Spanish onions

2 green bell peppers

4 cubanelle peppers

4 culantro leaves

10 ajíes dulces
(sweet peppers)

15 garlic cloves

1 tablespoon capers

If you take away one thing from this book, it is that *sofrito* is 100 percent, without a doubt, the most utilized staple in any Puerto Rican kitchen. This culantro-based sauce is truly the lifeblood behind Puerto Rican cuisine. You can buy Goya culantro-based Sofrito at the store or order it at most Puerto Rican restaurants, but nothing is better than making a fresh batch at home. The perfect blend of flavors makes anything from soups to sides to main courses something above and beyond anything you have ever tried.

Wash, peel, seed, and roughly chop the cilantro, bell pepper, Spanish onions, green bell peppers, cubanelle peppers, culantro leaves, ajies dulces, garlic cloves, and capers. Place the onions and cubanelle peppers in a food processor and pulse until finely chopped. Add the cilantro, red bell peppers, green bell peppers, culantro leaves, ajíes dulces, garlic, and capers in and continue blending until smooth.

SUBSTITUTION TIP: There are a couple of ingredients you may have trouble finding, but that's okay; there are simple substitutions. Cubanelle peppers can be replaced with green bell peppers, for a total of 6. If you can't find culantro, add in a little extra cilantro. Ajíes dulces can be replaced with Italian sweet peppers.

STORAGE TIP: I always make plenty of sofrito at a time so I have some on hand whenever I need it. I pour the extra Sofrito into an ice cube tray and freeze it, and I take the cubes and toss them right into whatever I'm making (each cube in my tray is about 2 tablespoons, but yours may be different).

Achiote Oil

MAKES: 1 cup | **COOK TIME:** 15 minutes

1 cup olive oil

4 tablespoons annatto seeds

When I first attempted to make arroz con gandules, I was certain that the orange hue of the rice came from tomato sauce. I later came to find out (and man, am I glad I did) that the color comes from achiote oil mixed into the rice. One of the greatest cooking lessons my father ever taught me was how to reduce annatto seeds into an oil that's used as a staple in many Puerto Rican recipes. This simple seed is probably one of the greatest secret weapons in the Puerto Rican cupboard.

1. Pour oil and seeds into a saucepan. Bring the oil to a slight simmer over medium heat, then turn the heat down to low and simmer for 2 to 3 minutes. Once the oil has taken on a deep red color, remove from heat.

2. Let oil cool to room temperature, then strain the seeds and discard.

STORAGE TIP: Store oil in a sealed jar at room temperature. Achiote will last for 2 to 3 months when properly stored.

Chicharrónes

Fried Pork Rinds/Crackling

MAKES: 10 servings | **PREP TIME:** 35 minutes | **COOK TIME:** 3 hours 30 minutes

3 pounds pork back fat with skin

2 cups oil

Salt

Pepper

It took me several years of cooking to realize when someone says *chicharrónes*, they're talking about one of two possible ways to make it. Each version has its own specific uses. This first one, an exploded pork crackling with little to no meat, is generally used in the making of other recipes, like Mofongo, for example. Once crushed in the Mofongo, they lend the same kind of texture that breadcrumbs do in some traditional American recipes.

1. Preheat oven to 250°F. Cut the pork into roughly 2-inch-wide strips, then slice along the strip between the skin and the fat, removing the fat from the skin. Cut the strips into 2-by-2-inch cubes.

2. Place a wire rack on top of a baking sheet, lay the cubes fat side down on the wire rack. Bake for about 3 hours until the pork skin is completely dried out.

3. Heat about 1 inch of oil over medium heat in a pan or skillet on the stove top. Do not allow the oil to start bubbling, place the dried pork skin in oil in batches. Fry for 4 to 5 minutes, until the pork skin bubbles and starts to puff up.

4. Remove from oil and place on paper towels to drain excess oil. Salt and pepper pork rinds to taste.

SUBSTITUTION TIP: If you're short on time, chicharrónes can be substituted with store-bought pork rinds, but let's be honest, once you make them from scratch you will never buy them bagged again.

STORAGE TIP: These will keep in the refrigerator for 3 to 4 days.

Chicharrón de Cerdo

Fried Pork Belly

MAKES: 10 servings | **PREP TIME:** 1 hour | **COOK TIME:** 25 minutes

2 pounds pork belly

1½ tablespoons
garlic powder

1½ teaspoons sazón
(see page 121)

1 teaspoon oregano

Salt

Pepper

2 cups oil

The second type of chicharrónes you'll come across is fried pork belly. While the first type can be eaten as a snack or used in a recipe, I have only ever eaten this one as a snack or side dish. Whenever my dad would make any kind of pork dish, he would cut some extra pork and fry it in the pan with the rest of dinner and just eat the fried pork pieces as his own side dish. Think of this as bacon that you can eat with any meal at any time. Okay, you can eat bacon with any meal at any time, so imagine bacon but seasoned and packed with even more flavor, and that's chicharrón de cerdo.

1. Cut pork belly into 2-by-2-inch cubes and place in a large bowl. Add the garlic powder, sazón, oregano, salt, and pepper over the pork and toss to coat.

2. Heat about 1 inch of oil in a pan or skillet over medium to high heat. Fry seasoned pork chunks until they are a deep brown on all sides, about 10 minutes. Remove pork from the pan and place on paper towels to drain excess oil. Season with salt and pepper to taste and serve immediately.

Adobo

Puerto Rican Seasoned Salt

MAKES: 2 cups | **PREP TIME:** 5 minutes

⅓ cup oregano

½ cup garlic powder

4 tablespoons onion powder

4 tablespoons black pepper

4 tablespoons ground cumin

4 tablespoons paprika

4 tablespoons ground coriander

2 tablespoons turmeric

During my childhood, our house was often the meeting place for friends from school, and one object they always seemed to notice was the red-topped plastic container of Goya Adobo seasoning. Mankind has had a long love affair with all forms of salt, and adobo is the one you'll find in Puerto Rican kitchens. Adobo seasoning is amazingly versatile and can be used in nearly every recipe in this book, and almost every recipe *not* in this book. Always remember to salt to taste, and be careful not to overdo the adobo.

Whisk together the oregano, garlic powder, onion powder, black pepper, ground cumin, paprika, coriander, and turmeric in a medium-size bowl.

STORAGE TIP: Store in a mason jar in a cool, dry place until ready to use. Adobo will last for well over a year.

Sazón

MAKES: ⅓ cup | **PREP TIME:** 5 minutes

- 1 tablespoon ground annatto seeds
- 1 tablespoon ground coriander
- 1 tablespoon cumin
- 1 tablespoon garlic powder
- 1 tablespoon salt
- 2 teaspoons oregano

Sazón, which literally translates to "seasoning," is as integral to the Puerto Rican kitchen as the star is to the Puerto Rican flag. One does not exist without the other. What often amazes many people who have tasted my cooking or tried my recipes over the years is the robust flavors that Puerto Rican food contains. Once prepared, your sazón will be one of the most important tools in your kitchen, and don't be surprised how often you find yourself sprinkling this seasoning on a variety of dishes.

Whisk together ground annatto seeds, coriander, cumin, garlic powder, salt, and oregano in a medium-size bowl.

STORAGE TIP: Store in a mason jar in a cool, dry place until ready to use. Like most dried seasonings, sazón will last for well over a year.

Mojo Criollo

Garlic Marinade

MAKES: 2½ cups | **PREP TIME:** 15 minutes | **COOK TIME:** 10 minutes

½ cup olive oil

10 smashed and peeled
  garlic cloves

1½ cups orange juice

½ cup lime juice

½ cup lemon juice

2 jalapeños, sliced

Salt

Mojo Criollo is an amazing marinade that you can use on nearly every type of meat or seafood. As I thought about which staples I should cover in this chapter, I realized I had a bag of chicken thighs in my refrigerator right then, lazily resting on a jar of Mojo Criollo. I'm sure we've all heard the English slang word "mojo"—well, this is basically the Creole Mojo, so go ahead and get creative with your usage. Not just a marinade, it can be used as a salad dressing, a sandwich spread, or a dip for tostones for a blast of flavor.

1. Heat the oil in a saute pan or skillet over medium heat. Add the garlic and sauté for 1 to 2 minutes until the garlic becomes fragrant.

2. Add the orange juice, lime juice, lemon juice, jalapeños, and salt, and cook for 2 to 3 minutes, then remove from heat.

VARIATION TIP: If you prefer a smoother texture, simply pulse in a blender or food processor until smooth.

STORAGE TIP: Mojo Criollo will keep in the refrigerator, covered, for 3 to 4 days.

Picadillo de Carne

Beef Hash

MAKES: 5 servings | **PREP TIME:** 5 minutes | **COOK TIME:** 30 minutes

---

2 tablespoons achiote oil (see page 117)

¼ cup sofrito (see page 116)

¼ cup alcaparrado (see page 124)

1 pound ground beef

2 tablespoons tomato paste

Salt

Pepper

My *Picadillo de Carne* is one of the most versatile recipes that you'll find in this cookbook. From Pastelillos de Carne to Carne con Arroz y Habichuelas, or simply spooned over some eggs, this amazing ground beef recipe works in almost any dish. It also smells so good that I'll sneak a spoonful to snack on while cooking it. Have fun with this one and try it with pasta, as the protein for a salad, or even in a bowl topped with pique (see page 126). No matter what you eat it with, picadillo is always a perfect choice.

1. Heat achiote oil in a large saute pan or skillet over medium heat. Add in sofrito and alcaparrado and cook for about 5 minutes; the sofrito should be simmering and the moisture just starting to evaporate.

2. Add ground beef, breaking it up in the pan, and brown it until most of the moisture evaporates. Stir in tomato paste and cook for 2 to 3 minutes. Remove from heat and add salt and pepper to taste.

VARIATION TIP: Make this recipe your own by adding any of the following before the ground beef is added: ½ cup diced onions, ½ cup diced green peppers, ½ cup chopped cilantro, or 2 chopped culantro leaves.

STORAGE TIP: Picadillo will keep in the refrigerator for 3 to 4 days.

Dairy-Free / Gluten-Free / Nut-Free / Vegan

Alcaparrado

Olives and Capers

MAKES: 2 cups | **PREP TIME:** 15 minutes

---

6 ounces pimento-stuffed
   green olives

3 ounces capers

½ cup red wine vinegar

2 tablespoons olive oil

Pepper

As with many cooking staples, there are times when it would be much easier to just head down to the grocery store and buy a jar of olives and capers in oil. When you see how effortless it is to make your own alcaparrado and how much better it tastes though, you may never go back to store bought. You'll see that it's used in many of the recipes in this book; it's simple to make and adds amazing flavor. Sometimes just leaving the mason jar of alcaparrado open in the kitchen entices the family to start lurking around to see what I'm cooking.

Roughly chop green olives and place in a mason jar. Add the capers, vinegar, olive oil, and pepper to the jar and shake well. Store in the refrigerator to allow the flavors to mingle.

STORAGE TIP: Sealed and refrigerated, alcaparrado will last for about 6 weeks.

Hot Pepper and Garlic Sauce

MAKES: 2 cups | **PREP TIME:** 15 minutes

6 jalapeños, seeded and chopped

8 to 10 garlic cloves, minced

6 peppercorns

¼ cup lime juice

½ cup olive oil

2 teaspoons salt

When some people think of Puerto Rican food, there's often a misconception that many of the spices have a lot of heat, as they do in Mexico or Peru. In fact, many Puerto Rican spices tend to be on the mild side. *Ajili Mojili* is one of the exceptions to this rule as it is often made with hotter spices than most other Puerto Rican sauces. This little gem is another of my brother's favorites, and he often uses a couple of habaneros in addition to the jalapeños to kick it up a notch.

Put the jalapenos, garlic cloves, peppercorns, lime juice, olive oil, and salt into a food processor and blend until smooth. Seal in a jar and refrigerate.

STORAGE TIP: Ajili Mojili will keep in the refrigerator for 3 to 4 days.

Pique

Puerto Rican Hot Sauce

MAKES: 2 cups | **PREP TIME:** 15 minutes plus 2 days resting

---

5 habanero peppers

5 jalapeño peppers

1 Spanish onion, sliced

10 garlic cloves, halved and mashed

10 peppercorns

⅓ teaspoon salt

1 cup apple cider vinegar (extra if needed to fill your jar)

If you've ever eaten in a Puerto Rican restaurant, pique is the little jar of hot sauce that's likely to be on every table. Various pickled peppers (depending on how hot you like it) and garlic give it that perfect punch of flavor. You can drizzle this over nearly every recipe in this book and you'll find that it tastes a little different with each dish. When adding to a meal, you can use just the juice by holding a fork over the top of the jar, or if you like heat, get adventurous and go for the peppers, too.

1. Remove the stems from the habanero peppers and jalapeno peppers and quarter them lengthwise (do not remove the seeds).

2. Place peppers in a large jar and add onions, garlic, peppercorns, and salt. Fill the rest of the jar with apple cider vinegar leaving about ½ inch of space between the vinegar and the top of the jar. Close the jar tightly and shake to combine all the ingredients. Allow to sit for at least 2 days at room temperature.

STORAGE TIP: Pique will keep for a couple of months when refrigerated in a sealed container.

SUBSTITUTION TIP: Traditionally this is made with ají caballeros, but I know those can be difficult to find. In their place, you can use habaneros.

VARIATION TIP: I use a 50/50 split of habaneros and jalapeños. You can increase the heat by using more habaneros than jalapeños, or decrease the heat by using more jalapeños than habaneros.

Mojito

Garlic Dipping Sauce

MAKES: 2½ cups | **PREP TIME:** 15 minutes

1 cup olive oil

8 to 10 garlic
  cloves, minced

1 Spanish onion, chopped

3 tablespoons
  chopped cilantro

2 tablespoons lemon juice

2 tablespoons lime juice

Salt

Technically this is called a garlic *dipping* sauce, but my favorite way to use this *Mojito* is to drizzle it over mofongo and a little bit of lobster. You've probably noticed by now that Puerto Rican cuisine leans very heavily on the flavors garlic brings to the table, so it's only logical that we would have a recipe for garlic dipping sauce. This is perfect to eat with tostones to add a splash of flavor to the fried plantains. You can even brush a little bit of this across the top of a Jibarito to really bring your sandwich to the next level.

Put the olive oil, garlic cloves, onion, cilantro, lemon juice, lime juice, and salt in a food processor and blend until smooth. Seal in a jar and refrigerate.

STORAGE TIP: Mojito will keep in the refrigerator for 3 to 4 days.

INGREDIENT TIP: This garlic dipping sauce is not to be confused with Mojo de Ajo/Garlic Sauce. To make Mojo de Ajo, place 1 cup of oil and 10 peeled and crushed garlic cloves in a small saucepan and simmer for about 20 minutes. Once cool, blend in a food processor until smooth.

Salsa Rosa

Pink Sauce

MAKES: 1½ cups | **PREP TIME:** 10 minutes

1 cup mayonnaise

6 tablespoons ketchup

1 garlic clove, minced

Salsa Rosa is a fun little dipping sauce that many of us "invented" as children with a simple ketchup and mayo mixture; that is, until we learned how much more amazing everything is with a little added garlic. Many Puerto Rican restaurants serve this as a dipping sauce and possibly call it by a different name. Sometimes I've even referred to it as "Mayo Ketchup Garlic Sauce." While the name may not be the most creative, what you can find to dip into Salsa Rosa is left to your imagination.

In a small bowl, whisk the mayonnaise, ketchup, and garlic clove together. Place in a mason jar, seal, and refrigerate until you are ready to use.

VARIATION TIP: Add in hot sauce or a little salt and pepper to taste until you get the flavor or heat you want.

STORAGE TIP: Salsa Rosa will keep in the refrigerator, covered, for 3 to 4 days.

Mojito Isleño

Island Sauce Dip

MAKES: 3½ cups | **PREP TIME:** 5 minutes

¼ cup olive oil

1 Spanish onion, chopped

1 green pepper, chopped

4 garlic cloves, minced

½ cup alcaparrado
  (see page 124)

1 cup tomato sauce

1 bunch cilantro

Salt

Pepper

In this book, I haven't gone too deeply into the fish recipes that bless the island, but if there is one thing to know about Puerto Rican fish recipes, it's that almost all of them can be topped with *mojito isleño*. This sauce goes perfectly with any type of fish, shrimp, scallops, and basically any other type of seafood. Topping grilled fish with mojito isleño is perfect for those looking for an amazingly simple sauce with immense flavor and very few calories.

1. In a saute pan or skillet, heat the oil over medium heat. Sauté the onions and bell peppers until onions start to become translucent.

2. Add garlic, and cook until the garlic becomes fragrant. Add in the alcaparrado, tomato sauce, cilantro, salt, and pepper and cook for another 10 minutes.

VARIATION TIP: If you want a little heat in your Mojito Isleño, go ahead and add some pique to your taste.

STORAGE TIP: Mojito Isleño will keep in the refrigerator, covered, for 3 to 4 days.

Dairy-Free / Gluten-Free / Nut-Free / Vegan

Chimichurri

MAKES: 1 cup | **PREP TIME:** 5 minutes

½ cup finely chopped cilantro

½ cup finely chopped parsley

2 tablespoons oregano

3 tablespoons minced red onion

1 tablespoon minced garlic

⅛ teaspoon adobo

Olive oil

While not a classic Puerto Rican recipe, chimichurri marries well with many of our dishes. This traditionally Central American sauce has found its way onto our little island. Many Puerto Rican restaurants serve this over their churrasco or have a bottle of it on the tables. This bright, tangy sauce has amazing flavor and is incredibly versatile as it can be used as a marinade, salad dressing, veggie dip, or as a topping for any kind of meat or seafood.

In a small bowl, mix the cilantro, parsley, oregano, onions, garlic, and adobo, then drizzle in a little olive oil, stirring until completely combined.

STORAGE TIP: Chimichurri will keep for about 3 days when covered and refrigerated.

Preparing Plantain/Banana Leaves

MAKES: 10 to 20 leaves | **PREP TIME:** 5 minutes | **COOK TIME:** 10 minutes

**10 to 20 plantain/
banana leaves**

I learned the hard way that you can't buy plantain or banana leaves from the store and expect to use them right out of the package to wrap anything. The first time I made Pasteles, my dad sat back and watched me struggle to wrap them because the leaves are very crisp and not at all pliable until you cook them. They kept splitting and cracking open, leaking all the hard work I had put into my Pasteles out onto my countertop. Over time, with practice and a healthy dose of listening to my dad laugh, I found that the 10 minutes of time spent cooking the leaves saved me hours of aggravation.

1. Preheat oven to 200°F. Cut the leaves to the size you need; this will vary depending on the recipe. Pasteles will need a larger-size leaf, while Guanimes need a much smaller-size leaf.

2. Place leaves on a baking sheet in a single layer, careful not to overlap them. Bake for 5 to 10 minutes, until the leaves are soft and pliable. Use immediately after preparing.

COOKING TIP: You can prep the leaves on the stove top by turning on one of the burners and slowly passing the leaf about 1 to 1½ inches above the flame. The leaves will darken to a deep green, but you don't want to burn them. Heat them just enough to make them pliable.

INGREDIENT TIP: If you want to give any of the dishes in this book a real island look and feel, line your serving plates with banana leaves; simply cut the leaf to the size of your plate before you serve your dish.

Measurement Conversions

VOLUME EQUIVALENTS (LIQUID)

US STANDARD	US STANDARD (OUNCES)	METRIC (APPROXIMATE)
2 tablespoons	1 fl. oz.	30 mL
¼ cup	2 fl. oz.	60 mL
½ cup	4 fl. oz.	120 mL
1 cup	8 fl. oz.	240 mL
1½ cups	12 fl. oz.	355 mL
2 cups or 1 pint	16 fl. oz.	475 mL
4 cups or 1 quart	32 fl. oz.	1 L
1 gallon	128 fl. oz.	4 L

OVEN TEMPERATURES

FAHRENHEIT (F)	CELSIUS (C) (APPROXIMATE)
250° F	120° C
300° F	150° C
325° F	165° C
350° F	180° C
375° F	190° C
400° F	200° C
425° F	220° C
450° F	230° C

VOLUME EQUIVALENTS (DRY)

US STANDARD	METRIC (APPROXIMATE)
⅛ teaspoon	0.5 mL
¼ teaspoon	1 mL
½ teaspoon	2 mL
¾ teaspoon	4 mL
1 teaspoon	5 mL
1 tablespoon	15 mL
¼ cup	59 mL
⅓ cup	79 mL
½ cup	118 mL
⅔ cup	156 mL
¾ cup	177 mL
1 cup	235 mL
2 cups or 1 pint	475 mL
3 cups	700 mL
4 cups or 1 quart	1 L

WEIGHT EQUIVALENTS

US STANDARD	METRIC (APPROXIMATE)
½ ounce	15 g
1 ounce	30 g
2 ounces	60 g
4 ounces	115 g
8 ounces	225 g
12 ounces	340 g
16 ounces or 1 pound	455 g

Index

Acknowledgments

Thank you to my father, Rafael, for helping me connect with our Puerto Rican heritage and for the hours he spent laughing in the kitchen while teaching me to cook. Thank you to my mom, Patty, for keeping me on the straight and narrow for many years and never giving up on me. And my little brother, Dennis, without whom this book wouldn't be possible. You helped me perfect family recipes, you helped me when I was at a loss for words, and you helped me network and grow. To my children, Anthony and Maddie, who amaze me every day and give me purpose. Last but not least, most importantly, thank you to Katie, my wife, who has been my rock and support through thick and thin, who put up with my making messes in the kitchen while I worked at my craft. Without her, the Average Guy Gourmet, this book, nothing I have done would have been possible.

About the Author

TONY RICAN is the creator of "Average Guy Gourmet," a YouTube cooking channel with nearly 15,000 subscribers, built around simple and fun recipes created by an average dad. With his family originally from Santurce, Puerto Rico, Tony was the first generation born off the island after his father moved to Chicago. He spent 15 years on the road as a professional wrestler and has since settled down to become a husband and a father. His greatest accomplishment—becoming a dad—is what made him want to reconnect with his heritage and explore Puerto Rican culture through its cuisine, with his father and children. He now uses the theatrics and production he learned from pro wrestling, along with simple meals taught to him by his father, to help others learn to cook. Visit him online at AverageGuyGourmet.com.

Printed in the USA
CPSIA information can be obtained
at www.ICGtesting.com
LVHW060409120124
768705LV00003B/22

9 781646 118038